# RECREATION MANAGEMENT
# OF WATER RESOURCES

# RECREATION MANAGEMENT OF WATER RESOURCES c.1

**Phillip Rea**
**Roger Warren**
*North Carolina State University*

Publishing Horizons, Inc., Columbus, Ohio

1    2    3    4  ⚐  7    6    5    4

**Library of Congress Cataloging-in-Publication Data**

Warren, Roger, 1932-
　　Recreation management of water resources.

　　Bibliography: p.
　　1. Outdoor recreation—United States—Management. 2. Aquatic sports—United States —Management.
3. Water resources development—United States.
I. Rea, Philip. II. Title.
GV191.67.W3W37　　1986　　333.78'4　　86-628
ISBN 0-942280-28-8 (soft)

# CONTENTS

# PREFACE

Americans annually flock to ocean and lake beaches to swim and sunbathe; to lakes, ponds, sounds, and bays to fish, boat, sail, and waterski; to streams and rivers to raft, canoe, and kayak. A 1985 Gallup poll indicated that swimming and fishing ranked first and second as the most popular adult sport and recreation activities in the United States. The list of additional popular activities included motorboating, canoeing, rowing, waterskiing, and sailing.

Public park and recreation agencies at all levels of government, private utility companies, industries, and private individuals all must be good stewards of our nation's recreational water resources if we are to provide maximum public benefit and increase the enjoyment of people who use these resources. All of these groups own or have jurisdiction over landholdings that include ponds, lakes, streams, and rivers with great recreation potential.

This book is the second in a series of two books dealing with management of aquatic facilities and resources. The first, *Swimming Pool Management,* was published in 1985 and focuses on the problems associated with the management of public and private swimming pools. *Recreation Management of Water Resources* looks at management problems associated with lakes, beaches, streams and rivers. The books are designed to meet the needs of two groups. First, these books are useful to college students majoring in recreation and park administration who need to be knowledgeable about the area of aquatic management. Second, they are also designed to be used by the pool manager or lake manager who has more narrowly defined areas of responsibility.

It is our intent to provide the principles, guidelines and practical management tools for managing water resources effectively and efficiently with the goal of providing a safe, high-quality experience for the recreation user. We hope our readers will be good stewards of these valuable resources and that the management suggestions contained herein will help achieve that end.

Throughout this book, the impersonal pronouns *he, him,* and *his* have been used for both reasons of style and accepted English usage. In all cases we realize that the terms *she, her,* and *hers* could have been used.

We wish to express our appreciation to park and recreation agencies in Boynton Beach, Miami, and Palm Beach County, Florida, and both the city and county of Los Angeles, California, for providing material relative to their respective marina and beach operations.

# INTRODUCTION

## PARTICIPATION IN WATER-BASED ACTIVITIES

Water-oriented activities make a vital contribution to the field of outdoor recreation. Many studies, which have examined recreation participation and the demand for recreation areas and facilities, list swimming, boating, fishing, and waterskiing as highly popular activities. The first comprehensive study of recreation in the United States was the Outdoor Recreation Review Commission Report in 1962. This report indicated that water was a prime factor in most outdoor recreation activities. The surveys conducted for this report indicated that 44 percent of the population preferred water-based recreation over any other. There is no reason to believe the popularity of these activities is diminishing. In fact, lists of the fastest growing outdoor recreation activities consistently name sailing, waterskiing, and canoeing. Table 1.1 provides a listing of popular water-based activities in the United States; the percentage of people participating in the activities are given.

TABLE 1.1 *Participation in Selected Water-Based Recreation Activities.*

| Activity | Percentage Participating at Least One Time per Year | Percentage Participating Five or More Times per Year |
|---|---|---|
| Pool Swimming and Sunbathing | 63 | 49 |
| Fishing | 53 | 36 |
| Nonpool Swimming and Sunbathing | 46 | 35 |
| Boating | 34 | 20 |
| Canoeing, Kayaking, or Riverrunning | 16 | 5 |
| Waterskiing | 16 | 8 |
| Sailing | 11 | 5 |

*Source: The Third Nationwide Outdoor Recreation Plan: The Assessment.* Washington, D.C.: U.S. Department of the Interior, 1979.

In addition to those activities that take place in or on water, water also enhances outdoor recreation on land. The ideal site for a campsite or picnic table is on a lakeshore, beside a stream or river, or close to the ocean. A pond or marsh enhances nature study and provides an interesting and attractive location for photographers. A jogging or bicycle path adjacent to a river, pond, or lake makes those activities more pleasing to the participant.

PHOTO 1.1  *Windsurfing is growing rapidly in popularity.*

Photo courtesy of Metro Dade County Park and Recreation Department.

## AVAILABILITY OF WATER RESOURCES

Because there are approximately 108 million acres of water surface in the United States, Americans in most sections of the country are fortunate to have excellent water resources available. Fifty-five percent of these waters are inland while the remaining 45 percent are coastal (excluding the coastal waters of Hawaii and Alaska). The largest percentage of these waters are in the North (52 percent); another large portion is in the South (22 percent); and the remainder is divided among the Rocky Mountain, Great Plains, and the Pacific Coast regions.

Millions of Americans head for the beach each summer. Many own private cottages on the beach or at beach resorts that are close to the ocean, one of the Great Lakes, or the Gulf coast. In some sections of the United States, public access to these beach areas is severely limited. In only a very few areas is there good public access. Although there are nearly 37,000 miles of shoreline along the coast of the contiguous forty-eight states, at least 70 percent of it is

PHOTO 1.2 *Water enhances other recreation activities, for example, a concert.*

Photo courtesy of United McGill Corporation, Columbus, Ohio.

in private ownership and only 25 percent of the total shoreline is available for recreation use. Table 1.2 indicated the ownership and use of United States coastal shoreline according to a 1971 study by the U.S. Army Corps of Engineers.

Prior to 1960 only one national seashore, Cape Hatteras in North Carolina, had been established. During the 1960s Cape Cod (Massachusetts, 1961); Point Reyes (California, 1962); Padre Island (Texas, 1962); Fire Island (New York, 1964); Assateague Island (Maryland and

TABLE 1.2 *Ownership and Use of United States Coastal Shoreline (Excluding Alaska), 1971.*

| Ownership | Miles of Shoreline | Percent |
|---|---|---|
| Federal | 3,900 | 11% |
| State and Local | 4,600 | 12 |
| Private | 25,800 | 70 |
| Uncertain | 2,600 | 7 |
| Total | 36,900 | 100 |
| **Use** | | |
| Recreation, Public | 3,400 | 9 |
| Recreation, Private | 5,800 | 16 |
| Nonrecreation | 27,700 | 75 |
| Total | 36,900 | 100 |

Virginia, 1965); Cape Lookout (North Carolina, 1966); Indiana Dunes (Indiana, 1966); and Pictured Rocks (Michigan, 1966) were all established as national seashores.


## Legislative Acts

In an effort to further protect the nation's coastline and estuaries from residential and commercial development, the Coastal Zone Management Act of 1972 was passed. The act had as its primary purpose, "to preserve, protect, develop, and where possible, to restore and enhance, the resources of the Nation's Coastal Zone for this and succeeding generations."

The Coastal Zone Management Program is administered by the Commerce Department, National Oceanic and Atmospheric Administration. The program provided grants to states to develop Coastal Zone Management Plans. Amendments to the act in 1976 provided for a beach access program. The primary responsibility for carrying out the Coastal Zone Management Programs remains with the various states.

The nearly two million rivers and streams in the United States provide Americans with another valuable water-based recreation resource. These rivers and streams total 3.2 million linear miles. Some are small streams that provide opportunities for fishing only, while others are expanses of open water that can be utilized for a complete mix of recreation activities. In the past many of these rivers and streams were unusable for recreation because of pollution. Recent legislation aimed at improving water quality has been successful, and water-based river recreation opportunities have been restored on many rivers and streams throughout the United States.

The National Wild and Scenic Rivers Act (1968) was passed in an attempt to preserve selected rivers for the enjoyment of present and future generations. The act established a system of protection for three classifications of rivers:

1. Wild Rivers—those rivers or sections of rivers that are free of impoundments and generally inaccessible except by trail, with shoreline and surrounding watershed essentially undeveloped. These rivers are unpolluted.
2. Scenic Rivers—those rivers or sections of rivers that are free of impoundments, with shorelines largely undeveloped. These rivers are accessible in some areas by road.
3. Recreation Rivers—those rivers or sections of rivers that are readily accessible, that may have some existing development along their shoreline, and that may have undergone some impoundment or diversion in the past.

The intent of the National Wild and Scenic Rivers Act was to preserve selected rivers or segments in their current condition by controlling new development. Eight rivers were designated by the original act. The eight rivers or sections of rivers were: Clearwater (Middle Fork), Idaho; Eleven Point, Missouri; Feather, California; Rio Grande, New Mexico; Rogue, Oregon; St. Croix, Minnesota and Wisconsin; Salmon (Middle Fork), Idaho; Wolf, Wisconsin. Many states have also adopted their versions of the act. Rivers continue to be studied for inclusion under state and federal programs. The availability of these resources has brought extensive interest and participation in canoeing, kayaking and rafting. Despite excellent potential for recreation, access to and recreation development on river shorelines has been extremely limited in many sections of the country. Only in recent years has there been an interest by towns and cities to develop waterfront areas for recreation use. We expect this trend to continue at an accelerated pace.

During the 1940s, 50s, and 60s a large number of man-made lakes were built in this country for hydroelectric power by private power companies, Bureau of Reclamation, and the Tennessee Valley Authority, and for flood control by the Corps of Engineers. As a result of this development, over 99 percent of all Americans live within fifty miles of a freshwater lake that is open to the public for recreation. The availability of large lakes for recreation is discussed more extensively in Chapter 3.

## BOATING OWNERSHIP

One way of assessing the popularity of water-based recreation is to look at boater registration and boating industry figures. According to U.S. Coast Guard registrations and estimates of nonregistered boats, 67.2 million people participated in some type of boating activity in 1984. Estimates for the number of boats in use in 1984 vary between 13.5 and 15.7 million. Based upon boating industry estimates, the *growth* in the number of recreational boats owned in the United States is shown in Figure 1.1.

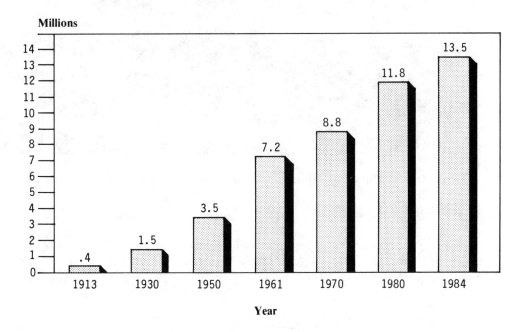

**FIGURE 1.1**   *Recreational Boats Owned in the United States (1913–1984)*

Boat ownership in 1984 is further broken down in Table 1.3.

**TABLE 1.3**   *Boat Ownership in 1984*

| Type of Boat Owned | Number |
|---|---|
| Outboard | 7,332,000 |
| Nonpowered Sailboats | 1,144,000 |
| Inboard/Outboard | 944,000 |
| Inboard | 431,000 |
| Open Deck | 111,000 |
| Houseboats | 29,500 |
| Canoes, Rowboats, Dinghies and Other Craft | 3,506,500 |
| Total | 13,498,000 |

Retail expenditures for the boating industry have risen from $2.5 billion in 1960 to $12.3 billion in 1984. A large percentage of this amount is accounted for in the number of boats sold: 657,730 in 1984. The fluctuation in the retail boating market can be illustrated by the number

PHOTO 1.3   *There is great demand for boating activity in heavily populated areas.*

Photo courtesy of Aqua-Matic Piers, Inc., Milwaukee, WI.

of sailboards sold. The first recorded sales of sailboards by the boating industry was in 1978 with 8,000 sold. This figure rose to 43,000 sailboards in 1984. By contrast, retail sales of outboard boats remained relatively constant for those years: 331,000 in 1978 and 317,000 in 1984.

## PROFESSIONAL ASSOCIATIONS

Interest in water-based recreation has spawned many organizations that promote and protect a variety of aquatic activities. The 1985 edition of *Encyclopedia of Associations* lists 196 such groups. Many of these organizations are highly specialized in their interest, for example, the Houseboat Association of America, the Snipe Class International Racing Association, the International Jet Ski Boating Association, and Bass 'N Gal (it promotes bass fishing). Some of these organizations are surprisingly large; for example, Snipe Class International Racing Association has 5,000 members and Bass 'N Gal has 7,500. Other organizations have a broader interest and have a major impact on water-based recreation in the United States. We have attempted to list and briefly describe some of the more prominent organizations and associations.

### American Canoe Association

Address:   7217 Lockport Place
           P.O. Box 248
           Lorton, VA 22079

The American Canoe Association, one of the oldest aquatic organizations, was founded in 1880. The purpose of this organization is to unite all persons interested in canoeing. It provides educational, informational, and training services to increase the enjoyment, safety, and skills of all canoeists at every skill level. One of its aims is to help conserve and preserve the natural environment and to improve access to the nation's canoeable waterways. The ACA is a member of both the United States Olympic Committee and the International Canoe Federation and serves as the governing body for national and international competition.

Members may participate in cruises, encampments, races and regattas, and training camps sponsored by the association. ACA publishes a bimonthly magazine and a newsletter, *The American Canoeist.*

## American Water Ski Association

Address:   799 Overlook Drive
           P.O. Box 191
           Winter Haven, FL 33882

Founded in 1939, the American Water Ski Association promotes water skiing at all levels of skill throughout the United States. The Association has its own official magazine, *The Water Skier.* As the governing body of organized water skiing in the United States, this organization sanctions more than 350 tournaments annually.

AWSA headquarters maintains skill ratings for all skiers who are eligible to enter sanctioned competition. It also keeps a current roster of more than 2,200 rated tournament judges, drivers, and scorers. Most AWSA members are active in some 400 affiliated water ski clubs which sponsor tournaments and water ski shows in many local areas of the United States.

## Boat Owners Association of the United States

Address:   880 S. Pickett Street
           Alexandria, VA 22304

Founded in 1966, this organization has a membership of more than 170,000 boat owners from throughout the United States. The organization represents a wide range of boater interests including cruising, racing, sport fishing, and waterskiing and includes owners of both power and sailing craft.

Activities of the organization include:

1.  Representation of boat owner interests before governmental legislative and regulatory bodies.
2.  Consumer Protection Bureau aiding in disputes between members, manufacturers, and boating suppliers.
3.  Membership services such as group-rate marine insurance, sale of publications and charts, seamanship and navigation correspondence courses, source for federal and state forms and regulations, and a bimonthly news journal.
4.  It supports BOAT/U.S. Foundation for Boating Safety which was established in 1979 to conduct research into recreational boating practices, usage, the causes of boating accidents, and to develop and disseminate new safety data, educational materials, and techniques to the boating community.

## Council for National Cooperation in Aquatics

Address:   P.O. Box 4724
           Evansville, IN 47711

Founded in 1951, the Council for National Cooperation in Aquatics is composed of representatives from thirty-three national organizations that are involved in water-based recreation activity. The organization provides a forum to share and discuss common problems, report on individual agency projects, and plan ways of working together. The Council sponsors aquatic research, conducts seminars and work groups, and provides demonstrations on swimming, boating, lifeguard training, swimming pool operations, skin and scuba diving, safety, protection, and maintenance of natural resources.

**National Association of Underwater Instructors**

Address:   4650 Arrow Highway, Suite F-1
P.O. Box 14650
Montclair, CA 91763

The National Association of Underwater Instructors (NAUI) was founded in 1960 and is the official training arm of the Underwater Society of America. NAUI is an association of professional diving educators; more than 10,000 instructors and leaders have successfully completed NAUI training programs. Their program has become international in scope. The organization offers an extensive series of skin and scuba diving programs.

**National Boating Federation**

Address:   2550 M Street N.W., Suite 425
Washington, DC: 20037

The National Boating Federation, founded in 1966, is an alliance of national, regional, and state recreational boating organizations. The goals of the National Boating Federation are as follows:

1. To represent, promote, and protect boating and related recreational activities and interests of recreational boaters at the national level.
2. To encourage programs of education and development; to conserve water resources for safer, more attractive boating; and to render assistance to member associations in the achievement of these objectives.
3. To provide a medium of exchange of boating information; to strive for unity among recreational boaters through their national, regional, and state associations; to provide a responsible voice in all matters affecting their interests, and to encourage boaters to organize into national, regional, or state associations for stronger, more effective representation.
4. To act as liaison among boaters, boating organizations, and federal and state agencies.

In addition to these goals or general objectives, the Federation more specifically actively promotes:

- Operator education but not operator licensing.
- Experienced waterway patrols to provide service and assistance.
- More and better aids to navigation.
- Higher safety standards for boats and equipment.
- Autonomy for state boating agencies and regular financing of their activities.
- Uniformity of boating laws and regulations.
- Practical control of litter and pollution.
- More and deeper waterways to facilitate safer navigation.
- Fewer lower-level fixed bridges and fairer drawbridge regulations to speed the flow of waterway traffic.
- More access sites and launching ramps, especially those close to urban areas. More marinas, marina berths, and waterway facilities.
- Government earmarking of boating revenues, including marine fuel taxes, for boating improvements.
- Better marine weather reporting.

**National Marine Manufacturers Association**

Address:   401 N. Michigan Avenue
Chicago, IL 60611

The National Marine Manufacturers Association was founded in 1979 by merger of several trade associations. This association represents the recreational boating industry and is composed primarily of manufacturers of boating products of all kinds. The organization owns and operates eight boat shows throughout the United States, engages in government relations activity, maintains a certification program for boats and other marine products, and engages in other activities to advance and promote the interest of its members. It also publishes statistical information on boating activity in the United States.

### National Safe Boating Council

Address:    Secretary NSBC, Inc.
            Comdt. (G-BBS), USCG-HQ
            2100 2nd Street S.W.
            Washington, DC 20593

The National Safe Boating Council, formed in 1958, is made up of organizations with a common interest in boating safety. These organizations consist of federal and state agencies directly involved in recreational boating safety and educational activities; national and regional nonprofit public service organizations involved in the recreation boating field; and national nonprofit boating industry organizations.

The Council's purpose is to provide a setting for national or regional nonprofit member organizations to advance and foster the safe enjoyment of recreational boating and to educate the public in the principles of safe boating with the goal of protecting life and property on the nation's waterways. The Council comes to public attention most during its annual sponsorship of National Safe Boating Week.

### Outboard Boating Club of America

Address:    2550 M Street, N.W., Suite 425
            Washington, DC 20037

The Outboard Boating Club of America is a charter member of the National Boating Federation. The primary function of the club is to keep its members informed about regulatory matters concerning recreational boating. It is a clearinghouse of information for individual small boat clubs located throughout the United States. Its principal service is a monthly newsletter, the *Legislative Ledger,* which chronicles what is happening in recreational boating legislation and rulemaking at all levels of government.

### Professional Association of Diving Instructors

Address:    1243 E. Warner Avenue
            Santa Ana, CA 92705

This organization organized in 1966 is a professional diving organization with over 16,000 instructors and more than 700 training facilities. It is an international organization which conducts training courses in many foreign countries. It publishes a variety of educational publications including materials devoted to diver training and instructor information, and management and operation of retail stores for diving equipment. It also publishes a magazine, *Diving Ventures.*

### Sport Fishing Institute

Address:    1010 Massachusetts Avenue, N.W., Suite 100
            Washington, DC 20001

Membership in this association is comprised of three groups who have a common interest in sport fishing as follows: (1) managers of fishery resources, (2) businesses that provide goods and services to sport fishermen, and (3) individual anglers. The Sports Fishing Institute was founded in 1949 by a group of sport fishing enthusiasts and fishing tackle manufacturers.

Goals and objectives of the Sport Fishing Institute include:

- Promoting and assisting in the conservation, development, and wise recreational use of our national fishery resources.
- Advancing and encouraging the development and application of all branches of fishery research and management.
- Collecting, evaluating, and publishing all valuable information for the advancement of fishery science and sport fishing.
- Assisting educational institutions in the training of fishery science and management personnel.
- Encouraging wider participation in sport fishing through the distribution of information pertaining to its health and recreation value.
- Assisting and encouraging cooperation between all existing conservation organizations.

The Sport Fishing Institute is recognized as a prime mover in helping to preserve and protect sound fishery management. The organization also represents the needs of recreational anglers through the legislative and regulatory process, establishing artificial reef programs, strongly supporting marine angling licenses, improving public access to underused waters, and promoting recreational fishing.

### United States Coast Guard Auxiliary

Address:   Commandant, United States Coast Guard
               U.S. Department of Transportation
               Washington, DC 20593

The U.S. Coast Guard Auxiliary was established by Congress in 1939 as a nonmilitary, volunteer affiliate of the U.S. Coast Guard. It was originally called the Coast Guard Reserve and was renamed the Coast Guard Auxiliary in 1941. The Auxiliary's basic mission is to assist the Coast Guard in promoting safe boating. Members must be at least seventeen years of age; own at least 25 percent interest in a boat, yacht, amateur radio station, or aircraft; or have special qualifications useful in the Auxiliary.

The stated aims of the Auxiliary are as follows: "To promote efficiency in the operation of motorboats and yachts. To foster knowledge of and better compliance with the laws, rules, and regulations governing the operation of motorboats. To facilitate other operations of the U.S. Coast Guard."

The Auxiliary does an excellent job of public education. It offers several different courses to the public including Sailing and Seamanship, Coastal Piloting, Boating Skills and Seamanship, and several other short courses. Courses are designed for the beginner and cover such subjects as aids to navigation, rules of the road, small boat maneuvering, charts and compass, and weather. Courses are normally free except for books and instructional materials. In some localities these courses have been taught in secondary schools and through the use of public television.

A second major program of the Auxiliary is Courtesy Marine Examination. Specially qualified members are authorized as courtesy examiners to conduct Courtesy Marine Examinations on recreational boats when requested by the owner or operator. These examinations embrace all the safety requirements of federal law, state law, and additional standards for safety which have been adopted by the Auxiliary. No report is made to any law enforcement agency if a boat fails to pass. If the boat passes, it is awarded a distinctive decal which signifies that the boat has met Auxiliary standards. This decal will normally exempt the boat from routine state or local boarding unless an obvious violation is evident.

### United States Power Squadrons

Address:   P.O. Box 30423
               Raleigh, NC 27622

Members of the Power Squadrons are pleasure boat owners and others interested in studying navigation and acquiring boating skills. They offer free instruction in safe boating to the public and courses in seamanship, advanced piloting, celestial navigation, marine electronics, engine maintenance, and weather to members.

### United States Rowing Association

Address:   251 N. Illinois Street, Suite 980
Indianapolis, IN 46204

The U.S. Rowing Association is the national governing body for rowing in the United States. Founded in 1872 as the National Association of Amateur Oarsmen, the name was changed in 1981 to reflect the broader purposes of the organization. It serves as a clearinghouse for rowing information, sells many publications and videotapes, and publishes a bimonthly magazine, *Rowing USA*. It promotes recreational rowing and also organizes regional and national championships for men, women, and master rowers. It also provides educational programs for coaches and judge-referees which may lead to licensing as a USRA judge-referee.

### United States Yacht Racing Union

Address:   P.O. Box 209
Newport, RI 02840

This is another of the older boating associations, founded in 1897. Its membership includes yacht clubs, associations, and individuals. This organization is the coordinating and governing body of sailboat racing in the United States, sponsoring twenty sailing championships each year. It maintains a speakers bureau and conducts specialized education programs.

## WATER SAFETY

As we indicated earlier in this chapter, millions of Americans enjoy water-based recreation each year. Unfortunately, a large number lose their lives while participating. Drowning is by far the leading cause of death while engaging in aquatic activities. In fact, drowning is the third leading cause of death in the United States. Only motor vehicle accidents and falls cause more fatalities. In 1983, 6,600 people lost their lives by drowning (see Figure 1.2). Not all of these

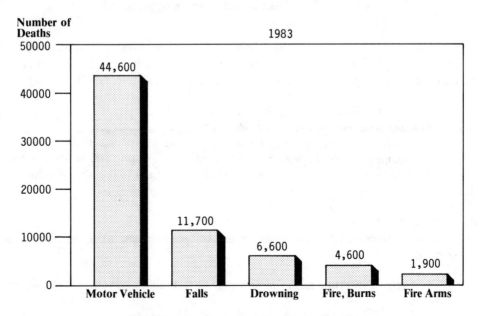

FIGURE 1.2  *Causes of Accidental Deaths*

people were engaged in a recreational activity. In a typical year there will be drownings because of incidents such as floods, automobile vehicles running off the road into bodies of water, and small children being left unattended in a bathtub. However, the great majority drown while swimming, boating, fishing, waterskiing, or walking near the water. Figure 1.3 graphically shows drowning accidents in the United States from 1900 to 1980. Figure 1.4 shows drowning deaths per 100,000 population. It is evident from these two illustrations that water safety efforts during the past twenty to thirty years have been effective in holding drowning at a reasonably low level. The historical reduction in deaths has come as a result of learn-to-swim programs and an overall effort by many organizations to emphasize the danger associated with water-oriented recreation activities.

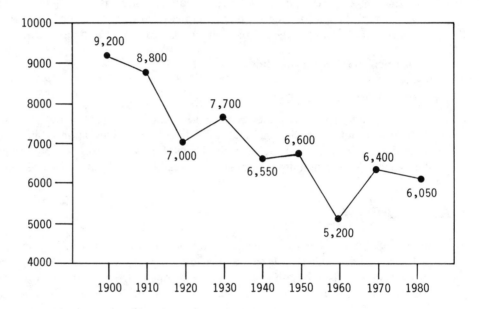

FIGURE 1.3  *Drowning Accidents*

Everyone associated with water-based recreation management needs to be aware of the danger of drowning accidents and make every effort to reduce the number of annual drownings even further. Efforts to reduce drowning accidents should include the following:

- See that children learn to swim at an early age.
- Teach swimming in the public schools.
- Support local and state legislation that will make aquatic activities safer.
- Communities should construct and operate safe boating and swimming facilities.
- Observe the water safety rules and regulations listed in the section below.

## Water Safety Rules

### General

1. Learn to swim and learn simple lifesaving techniques, so you can help someone in trouble.

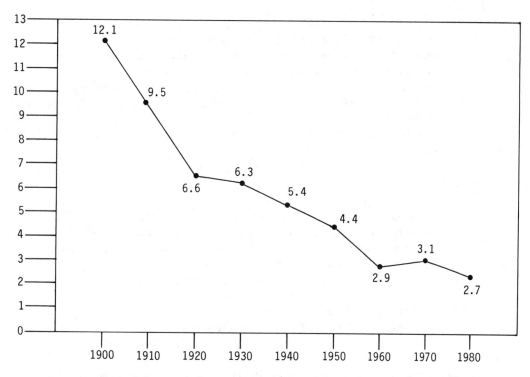

**FIGURE 1.4** *Drowning Deaths Per 100,000 Population*

2. Learn to administer CPR.
3. Do not go near the water when under the influence of alcohol.
4. Be aware that heavy boots and/or clothing are an extra hazard if you fall into the water.
5. Cold water is especially dangerous. Even a good swimmer can survive only a short time in 35- to 40-degree water.
6. Be sure that ice on a lake or pond is thick enough before walking or skating on it.
7. Do not skate on frozen rivers (there may be weak spots from the river's current).
8. Watch the weather on a large body of water. (In a storm, smooth water can quickly become very turbulent.)

*Swimming*

1. Never swim alone regardless of swimming ability.
2. Swim at an area that is supervised.
3. Private swimming areas should have safety equipment available, for example, a reaching pole or heaving line.
4. Do not wade in water where you are uncertain of the underwater contour.
5. Never swim during an electric storm.
6. Be especially careful in water with tides, currents, and heavy surf.
7. Distance swimming should be undertaken only with a boat accompanying the swimmer.
8. Nonswimmers should not rely on flotation devices in deep water.
9. Children should be warned of the danger around ponds, drainage ditches, quarries, and gravel pits.

*Boating*

1. Learn the "rules of the road" for the operation of a boat.
2. Nonswimmers should *wear* personal flotation devices when using a small craft.
3. Be certain the boat you are using can float when submerged.
4. Do not stand up in a small craft or in a motorboat when it is in gear.
5. Do not leave a capsized boat—wait until you are picked up or can paddle the submerged boat to shore.
6. Sit on the seat of a motorboat—never on the gunnel, bow, or transom when the motor is running.

*Waterskiing*

1. Know how to swim and wear a Type III personal flotation device.
2. Stay clear of solid objects, such as docks, piers, and bridge abutments.
3. Keep a reasonable distance from swimmers, fishermen, and other skiers.
4. Know and use the proper waterskiing signals.
5. Hold up a ski after a fall if other boats are operating nearby.
6. Do not ski at night.
7. Do not ski to the point of exhaustion.
8. Do not ski doubles with different length tow ropes.

## Boating Safety

The Federal Boating Act of 1958 required the U.S. Coast Guard to collect, analyze, and publish appropriate boating safety statistics. They have published these statistics each year since 1959. Table 1.4 shows boating fatalities for a twenty-year period 1964 to 1984.

**TABLE 1.4**  *Boating Fatalities 1964–1984*

| Year | Fatalities | Fatality Rate per 100,000 Boats |
|------|-----------|-------------------------------|
| 1964 | 1192 | 19.2 |
| 1965 | 1360 | 21.4 |
| 1966 | 1318 | 20.4 |
| 1967 | 1312 | 19.7 |
| 1968 | 1342 | 19.6 |
| 1969 | 1350 | 19.0 |
| 1970 | 1418 | 19.2 |
| 1971 | 1582 | 20.2 |
| 1972 | 1437 | 16.9 |
| 1973 | 1754 | 18.3 |
| 1974 | 1446 | 13.5 |
| 1975 | 1466 | 12.4 |
| 1976 | 1264 | 9.9 |
| 1977 | 1312 | 10.0 |
| 1978 | 1321 | 9.8 |
| 1979 | 1400 | 10.1 |
| 1980 | 1360 | 9.5 |
| 1981 | 1208 | 8.3 |
| 1982 | 1178 | 7.9 |
| 1983 | 1241 | 8.1 |
| 1984 | 1063 | 6.8 |

Although the number of fatalities has remained relatively constant during this twenty-year period, there has been a dramatic decrease in fatalities per 100,000 boats. This success can most likely be attributed to (1) more stringent safety laws at both the federal and state levels, (2) emphasis on boating safety during this period to condition boaters to be more safety conscious, and (3) education programs that improve boating operational skills and emphasize good safety practices.

Of the 1,063 fatalities that occurred in 1984, 37.2 percent were a result of the boat capsizing, 24.6 percent were a result of falling overboard, and 15.1 percent were a result of the boat colliding with another vessel, or a fixed or floating object. It should be noted that the cause of death in most of these instances was drowning; the type of accident refers only to the first event that occurred.

A boating accident report form has been developed by the U.S. Coast Guard. The operator of a boat is required to file a relatively complex report to the state where the accident occurred whenever a boating accident results in:

1. Loss of life.
2. Injury requiring medical treatment beyond first aid.
3. Property damage in access of $200 or complete loss of the vessel.

## SUMMARY

A major share of recreation activity takes place in, on, or near water. Millions of Americans head for lakes, streams, ponds, rivers, and ocean beaches consciously choosing to spend large portions of their leisure at these places. In this chapter we have attempted to indicate something of the scope of water-based recreation in the United States. We have shown that millions of people participate in a variety of water-based recreation activities. We have also shown that the supply of water-based recreation opportunities for most Americans is good. Unfortunately, many of the available and potentially available areas and facilities are poorly managed, and the quality of the participant's recreation experience suffers as a consequence.

The remainder of the book deals with management problems related to small lakes, large lakes, beaches, and marinas. There are a number of environmental and sociopolitical reasons why some aquatic areas and facilities may not be the very best. However. whether a facility is a $15 million marina or a boat rental operation on a small municipal lake, there is no excuse for poor management. Good management that provides the finest possible recreation experience for all participants must be the goal of the leisure services industry.

# 2

# SMALL LAKE MANAGEMENT

Water is an immensely popular feature in any recreation development. All water resources, from oceans to small ponds and streams, have a magnetic appeal that attract large numbers of people. Some people value water for its aesthetic qualities while others see a lake or stream as a potential recreation resource. The combined effect of aesthetic quality and recreation potential often result in the development of housing and business complexes that capitalize on water resources to set the tone for the project. Waterfront property has become so popular that the demand far exceeds the supply.

In general, the larger the water area, the greater the potential for recreation development. Activities such as water skiing and power boating require large bodies of water to assure a safe recreation experience. On the other hand, a small lake can accommodate a surprisingly large number of recreation pursuits in a safe and efficient manner. With proper planning, the small lake or pond can provide a wider range of recreation opportunities for its size than any other type of park facility. In addition, the small lake has the potential to generate revenue in excess of operating costs.

## PLANNING AND DESIGN

There are over 2½ million ponds and small lakes throughout the country. The Northeast and upper Midwest are fortunate to have numerous natural lakes in beautiful settings. However, in Southern areas of the United States, ponds and lakes must usually be constructed. In most cases the primary reason for constructing a pond or small lake is something other than recreation. It is certainly more common to find lakes of all sizes constructed to help solve an environmental problem than for aesthetic or recreation purposes. Lakes are usually constructed for flood control and water supply reasons, while ponds are usually constructed to provide water for irrigation or livestock, or to assist in erosion control. Nevertheless, most impoundments have recreation potential and oftentime, as far as the user is concerned, little thought is given to the primary reason the lake was constructed. Where recreation use will be permitted, the agency that is to assume responsibility for that function should have an active role in planning the lake.

An advantage in constructing small lakes for recreation is that some degree of control is possible on the eventual use and management of the entire impoundment. If more than one site is under consideration, factors such as accessibility, aesthetics, availability of utilities, and relationship of sites to population areas should receive attention. The following planning and design considerations for small lakes are recommended: (1) program, (2) location, (3) size, (4) site characteristics, (5) water control structures, and (6) additional facilitites. Each of these areas are discussed below.

## Program

One of the first steps in planning any recreation area is to determine the program, or proposed use, of the site. The more common small lake activities are boating, fishing, and swimming. Consideration should also be given to the encouragement of passive enjoyment of the lake environment. It is at the program determination stage that the question of revenue production should be considered. If, for example, it is the agency's desire for the lake to operate a boat rental operation at a profit to subsidize an interpretive program for which no fee will be charged, it is vital that correct decisions are made relative to the type and number of rental boats that will be provided. The question of revenue will be addressed in depth later in this chapter.

## Location

The location of the small lake operation is extremely important, particularly where financial self-sufficiency is a goal. While people are drawn to water features, it should not be assumed that every small lake has the potential of generating significant amounts of revenue. Most small lake activities that generate revenue are impulsive in nature. That is, the users are attracted to the area for a specific activity, such as a family picnic, and develop interest in the lake activities after observing others in rental boats, fishing, consuming snacks, etc. A small lake operation, by itself, may not be enough to attract users in sufficient numbers to generate the revenue necessary to cover operating costs. For that reason, the ideal location for a small lake operation with a revenue production emphasis is in a community- or regional-type park that will attract large numbers of visitors for picnicking, swimming, and other activities.

## Size

Because lake size is relative, there seems to be little agreement as to the importance of this factor in determining the definition of a small lake. The term *small lake* is used primarily by recreation planners and is identified as much by the type of activities permitted on the impoundment as its physical size. In areas of the country that have limited water resources, a small lake may be as small as one to several acres, a pond by another person's definition. For others, it may be an impoundment of several hundred acres. Most small lakes regulate the type of activities that will be permitted; e.g., boat and/or motor size, swimming, launching, etc. While the larger the lake, the greater the variety of activities that can be accommodated, an impoundment of just a few acres can support a large number of water-based pursuits. Additionally, the smaller the impoundment, the easier it usually is to control and maintain. For example, the manager of a ten-acre lake might be able to permit rental boats to use the entire impoundment, whereas on a larger lake, a zoning system may have to be developed that, in effect, limits the craft to an area of just a few acres.

## Site Characteristics

Proper selection of the small lake site will alleviate many potential management problems once the lake is put into operation. Three major factors must be considered when selecting the small lake site: (1) suitable topography, (2) acceptable soil type, and (3) water supply. The interaction of these factors will determine lake size, shape, depth, and life span. Additionally, potential problems associated with fisheries management, maintenance, and visitor control can be minimized or avoided.

*Topography.*   The ideal topography for the small lake site is a wide gently sloping basin that narrows at the proposed dam site. The objective is to create the largest possible impoundment area with the smallest dam.

There are numerous technical publications on general lake construction that are useful in planning the small lake. However, some modifications may be considered to maximize public usage, management efficiency, and general aesthetics. The *Manual and Survey on Small Lake Management* makes the following recommendations relative to topography and slope:

> It is common practice to construct lakes with a two-to-one outer slope on the dam, but a four or even five-to-one slope will blend into the topography better, help to hide the man-made touch, provide easier access and facilitate maintenance.
>
> A path, not usually found around farm ponds, is a necessity for public use. This should be wide enough to accommodate maintenance equipment. Ten feet is a good width and allows for the inevitable erosion of the shoreline by wave action. A shallow shelf is formed by this wave action, which acts as a breakwater, and erosion becomes negligible. (See Photo 2.1.)
>
> Paths should be kept to a maximum of one foot above water level. Less height is desirable... .
>
> Inner slopes should be established at a three-to-one ratio (a drop of one foot in three feet) to permit a depth of three feet to be reached as quickly as possible. By obtaining a depth below the zone of light penetration within a few feet of shore, water weeds can be limited to a narrow band around the shoreline greatly reducing the weed control problem. If the lake is built in a geographical area of severe winters and extended ice cover, minimum depth should be at least fifteen feet to prevent winter kill of fish.[1] (See Figure 2.1.)

If the small lake program includes fishing skills instruction, consideration should be given to the grading and landscaping of an area that will allow backcasting. This is particularly true of fly fishing. A relatively flat bank, free from trees and shrubs for a distance of forty to fifty feet and located away from intensively used areas, would be ideal for instructional purposes.

*Soil type.* It is important that the lake site contain enough clay to provide a watertight dam and basin with minimum seepage. If there is any doubt as to the ability of the proposed site to

**PHOTO 2.1** *Pathways constructed around recreation lakes and ponds accommodate users and maintenance equipment.*

Photograph provided by Wheeling Park, Wheeling, W.Va. Park Commission.

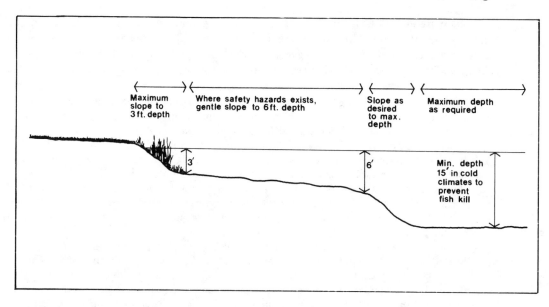

**FIGURE 2.1** *Inner slope and bottom contour should be constructed to minimize potential management problems.*

*Source: Lakes and Ponds,* The Urban Land Institute, Technical Bulletin No. 72.

sustain a relatively constant water level, consideration should be given to securing the services of a soil engineering consultant to evaluate the proposed lake bed. A soil survey, including the taking of a minimum of four soil borings per acre, should be made of the dam site and the entire potential lakebed.[2]

If the proposed lakebed consists of porous soils, gravel, or other sand, it may be necessary to transport clay or other waterproofing materials to the impoundment. Another alternative is to use impermeable PVC (polyvinylchloride) lining to prevent seepage. Rock outcroppings, shale ledges, and limestone areas should be avoided because these areas may lead to excessive seepage.

*Water supply.*    The water supply for small lakes and ponds is normally provided by a combination of three sources: springs, streams, and surface runoff. The actual impoundment is created through a combination of constructing a dam to control the flow and raise the level of the water, and grading or dredging to determine shape, size, and depth. If the impoundment is created by damming streams, difficulties usually arise in controlling the game fish population. Desired game fish may escape while rough fish enter through the lake's inlet. Lakes created from impounding springs, and with enough watershed to assume a constant water level, usually prove to be satisfactory.

The watershed should provide enough silt-free water to keep the lake full at all times with water seldom running over the spillway. A permanent cover of grass and other forms of vegetation in the watershed area are valuable in filtering polluted or sediment rich runoff before it flows into the lake.

The size of the watershed for a pond or lake depends primarily on the volume of the impoundment, rate of rainfall, topography of the watershed, and the usage of the watershed. These factors vary widely throughout the United States. Figure 2.2 is a general guide to estimating the approximate size of drainage area needed for ponds and small lakes. Technical assistance should be obtained from the Soil Conservation Service or a private engineer to confirm the accuracy of the ratio of watershed area to impoundment size for a specific site.

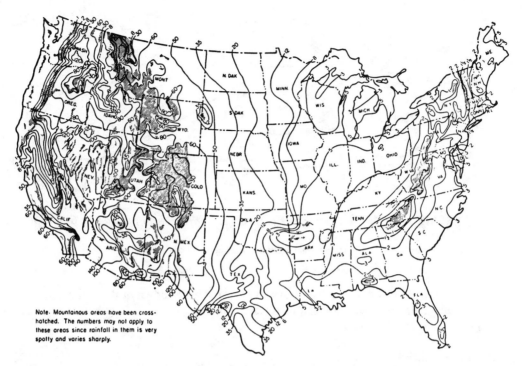

Note. Mountainous areas have been cross-hatched. The numbers may not apply to these areas since rainfall in them is very spotty and varies sharply.

FIGURE 2.2   *A guide for estimating the approximate size of drainage area (in acres) required for each acre-foot of storage in an embankment or excavated pond.*

*Source: Ponds for Water Supply and Recreation,* U.S. Dept. of Agriculture, Washington, D.C., 1971.

## Water Control Structures

Before construction begins, plans should be prepared for the design of the dam, spillway, and drain system. Again, the Soil Conservation Service as well as private engineers can provide the technical assistance necessary in preparing construction plans.

The dam should have a top width of at least ten feet. This width prevents serious damage from burrowing animals and provides structural integrity. The dam may need to be wider if it is to serve as a roadway.

No matter how well a dam is built, it will probably be damaged or destroyed if floodwaters are allowed to flow over the top. Protection of the dam from floodwaters should be provided by an emergency spillway. The function of an emergency spillway is to pass excess storm runoff to the streambed below the dam. Earthen spillways should be protected by grass or other vegetation; they should be wide enough to keep the flow shallow. This minimizes erosion and helps to keep large fish from swimming out of the lake. Do not screen the spillway to hold the fish. A screen traps trash as well as fish and ends the usefulness of the spillway.

In planning for lakes over ten acres in size, consideration should be given to the construction of an overflow pipe, or riser. Such a structure keeps the normal water level a few inches below the earthen spillway. The overflow or riser structure consists of a vertical pipe to control the water level and a drainpipe to empty the lake. (Figure 2.3)[3]

It is important that a method of draining the lake be included during the construction process. It may be necessary to drain the lake so that undesirable rough fish may be removed and a more desirable fish population can be established. It may also be used to draw down the water level in the fall so that many small bluegill or bream will be trapped in shoreline vegetation and those remaining will be more easily caught by bass, the most popular small lake game fish.

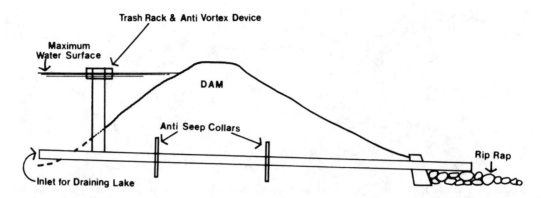

**FIGURE 2.3** *Overflow structure controls water level and provides a drain for lake.*

*Source: Lakes and Ponds,* The Urban Land Institute, Technical Bulletin No. 72.

Eventually it will also be necessary to draw the water down or drain the lake to facilitate the construction of docks or piers, or for dredging shoreline areas that have been taken out of use by siltation and aquatic weed growth.

## Additional Facilities

The major structures at a typical small lake operation are the boathouse and dock area. The boathouse is the control center from which boats are rented, refreshments are sold, and equipment is stored and repaired.

*Boathouse.*     The boathouse should be immediately adjacent to the rental boat dock to maximize the efficiency of the operation by minimizing the number of staff necessary to meet the users' needs. If the boathouse is removed from the dock area, an additional staff person may be necessary to collect the boater's ticket and provide assistance in entering and exiting the boats. During those days or hours when lake visitors are at a minimum, having the boathouse adjacent to the dock enables one or two staff persons to manage the entire operation.

The boathouse might also house restrooms, a drinking fountain, and possibly a sheltered sitting area from which the lake activity can be observed. In many cases the shelter makes an excellent off-season boat storage and repair area.

*Docks.*     The dock system for small lakes is usually a permanent structure attached to a concrete headwall. At lakes with fluctuating water levels or severe winter freezing, floating rather than permanent docks may be more practical (Photo 2.2).

Parking areas, walkways, and trails will also be required. The capacity of the parking lot will be related to the types of activities available at the lake site. If roadside parking is not permitted, the size of the parking lot will help determine the maximum number of visitors at any one time. Conversely, the number of rental boats, picnic tables, and other recreation opportunities will help determine the needed number of parking spaces. Table 2.1 reflects the number of people per car that can be expected at various types of activities typically found at a small lake.

Walkways connecting high-use areas (e.g., parking area to boathouse) may require a surfacing material to avoid erosion. This can be a critical problem at a small lake site, for eroded soil will surely be carried into the lake, eventually resulting in a buildup in shoreline siltation and weed growth. Bituminous material may be desirable on heavily used areas or at points of concentrated use. Crushed stone or fine gravel may be acceptable for lakeside paths.

Other areas and facilities, while not water-based, can be compatible with the small lake environment. Playgrounds, observation areas, miniature golf courses, and bike trails are just a

**PHOTO 2.2**  *Boathouse should be adjacent to dock for management efficiency.*

Photograph provided by Oglebay Park, Wheeling, W.Va.

**TABLE 2.1**  *Vehicular Capacities and Turnover Rates*

| Type of Activity | No. of People per Car | Average Turnover Rate per Car |
|---|---|---|
| Boat Concession | 3.5 | 2 |
| Family Picnicking | 4–6 | 2 |
| Group Picnic | 4.5 | 1 |
| Fishing | 2.5 | Variable |
| Beach Areas | 3.5–4.0 | 2 |
| Sightseeing | 3 | Variable |

*Source: Recreation Ready Reference,* U.S. Dept. of Agriculture, Washington, D.C., 1977.

few examples. Minature golf and bike rental concessions have revenue producing potential and can be controlled from the boathouse. This multiple-use concept enables the manager to maximize recreation opportunities and revenue production with a minimum of staff and facilities.

# ENVIRONMENTAL PROBLEMS IN SMALL LAKE MANAGEMENT

Beneath the still water of the small lake is a myriad of biological activity that, if not understood and acted upon, can lead to severe management problems, and possibly even the destruction of the impoundment. The planner as well as the manager of the impoundment must realize that lakes are transitory in nature. Simply put, that means they have a limited life span. In time, a lake gradually fills up with sediment carried from the surrounding watershed until the lake becomes dry land. This evolutionary process is natural and may take thousands of years. On the other hand, poorly planned lakes and lakes with mismanaged watersheds might only last fifteen to twenty years before they become unusable for water-based recreation.

New lakes are usually poor in nutrients and are called *oligotrophic*, while nutrient rich lakes are called *eutrophic*. Eutrophication is accelerated in temperate regions. Therefore, lakes in warmer climates age more rapidly than lakes in colder climates. Runoff from fertile lawns and agricultural land will be rich in nutrients and inorganic sediment, adding further acceleration to the eutrophication process. One of the consequences of the eutrophication process is a problem with aquatic weeds. Aquatic plants and algae normally take in carbon dioxide and expel oxygen. However, that process is reversed as aquatic vegetation dies and decomposes, a normal occurrence in the fall or even on cloudy summer days. Occasionally the consumption of oxygen by decomposing plants can deplete the oxygen supply in the lake and be significant enough to cause fish kills. This situation is particularly true in smaller impoundments with poor circulation, where water is subject to stratification. As winter approaches, the lake cools more rapidly at the surface than at lower levels. The cooler, heavier water sinks to the bottom, and the warm water at the bottom, together with much of the decomposing organic matter, rises to the surface and often causes unpleasant odors.[4] In northern climates where lakes are frozen over for months at a time, oxygen may be depleted from the water, causing fish to die of suffocation. This is particularly true of shallow lakes.

If not controlled, the combined effect of siltation and aquatic weed and algae growth can take a lake out of production. Unchecked weed growth can make fishing, boating, and swimming impossible.

## Sedimentation

To limit silt buildup, sediment eroding from land in the watershed area must be controlled. The primary factors in controlling sedimentation are as follows: (1) limiting erosion, and (2) slowing the flow of water down so that sediment can settle out of the water before it enters the lake.

Erosion can be limited through a variety of methods. Most important is to protect the soil in the watershed area with vegetation. Grass, trees, shrubs, and other plants will soften the effect of a hard rainfall while their root systems hold the existing soil in place.

Upstream construction often leads to sedimentation problems for water impoundments. Soil from unprotected construction sites can generate up to 100,000 tons of sediment per square mile per year, as compared to 100 tons per square mile per year from wooded countryside.[5]

Feeder streams should be examined to be sure they are not major contributors to siltation buildup in the small lake. Winding feeder streams with unprotected soil banks should be manipulated to minimize erosion. Covering steep banks with rock, or rip rap, will slow the erosion process considerably (Photo 2.3).

It may be advisable to consider the construction of a sediment pond or basin just upstream of the small lake. Such a structure will reduce the velocity of water flow, allowing much of the sediment to settle there rather than in the lake. A large, shallow pond with a spillway is effective in trapping much of the sediment while allowing clearer water to enter the main lake. The basin can be constructed to facilitate the regular removal of sediment deposits. While such structures add to the construction costs, they can add many years to the usefulness of a small lake. The Soil Conservation Service can provide technical assistance for the design and construction of sediment basins.

In those cases where sedimentation and aquatic weed growth has resulted in the small lake having limited value for recreation purposes, a decision will have to be made to either dredge or abandon the impoundment.

PHOTO 2.3   *Rip rap and vegetation minimizes bank erosion.*

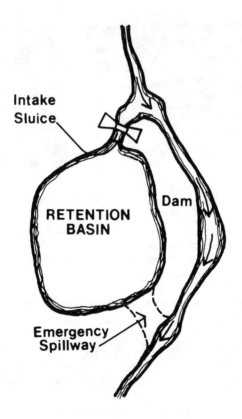

FIGURE 2.4   *A sediment retention basin can add years to the usefulness of a small lake.*

*Source: Lakes and Ponds,* The Urban Land Institute, Technical Bulletin No. 72.

While there are various ways to dredge lake bottoms, no method is easy nor inexpensive. If the lake can be drained, it may be possible to use heavy equipment to remove the years of sediment deposits. At least two other methods do not require the lake to be drained: (1) drag lines that work in strips traversing the lake and (2) barges with powerful suction engines that work very much like vacuum cleaners. Either method may require an adjacent deposit site to allow the dredged material to dry out before it can be trucked away. An alternative may be to create a small island in the lake from the excavated spoil. Once landscaped, such an island can add to the aesthetic beauty of the site and create a retreat for wildlife.

## Aquatic Weeds

Aquatic vegetation plays an important role in lake ecology. The presence of vegetation stimulates the growth of microorganisms, insect larvae, forage fish, and various aquatic animals. Fish do not eat the aquatic plants, but they do eat the animal life that feed on these tiny plants. Unfortunately, the proliferation of aquatic vegetation can become one of the biggest problems confronting the small lake manager. Left unchecked, water weeds can take whole lakes out of production, making them useless for recreation. It is impossible to fish and boats cannot navigate through weeds. Small fish find such good escape cover that larger fish cannot keep them in check. Reproduction of the small fish continues and soon the lake is full of stunted fish, too small to be of interest to the fisherman even if he could fish for them. Methods must be found to control this encroachment before it becomes a problem.[6]

PHOTO 2.4   *Mechanical aquatic weed cutters.*

*Mud Cat's aquatic weed harvester removes both floating and submerged weeds to restore the natural balance, preserve marine resources and protect fish and game habitats.*

*Hockney's underwater weed cutter is designed to cut and control any type weed that roots to the bottom.*

*Source:* Mud Cat Division of National Car Rental System, Inc., St. Louis Park, Minnesota.

Hockney Co., Silver Lake, Wisconsin.

It is easier to prevent most waterweeds from becoming established in a small lake than it is to get rid of them. Chemicals and manual removal are only temporary measures. The weeds will return unless conditions are made unfavorable for their growth. Fertile water and deep lake edges are the most effective and least expensive way to control most waterweeds.

## Fertilization

Fertilization increases the growth of microscopic plants. Fish each the worms, larvae, and other aquatic animals that feed on the tiny plants. It takes four to five pounds of these aquatic animals to produce a pound of bluegill or bream, and it takes four or five pounds of these small fish to produce a pound of bass. Thus, the high production of microscopic plants results in more pounds of fish. A highly fertile small lake can support as much as 300 to 400 pounds of fish per surface acre compared to about 150 to 200 pounds for an impoundment of normal fertility.[7]

The microscopic plants resulting from fertilization can also be of value in controlling submersed weeds. The microscopic plants, or planktonic algae, create a "bloom" which colors the water to a depth of eighteen inches or more, shading out plants growing from the lake bottom. Submersed waterweeds cannot grow without sunlight. Further, without weeds to harbor them, mosquito larvae are eaten by the fish.

It is difficult to determine when to fertilize ponds and small lakes and how much fertilizer to use. New ponds may benefit from fertilization in that the start of aquatic weed growth can be minimized and an abundant food source will develop for the rapid growth of stocked fish. From that point on, the best times to fertilize are in the spring and fall when fish are feeding heavily and experience maximum growth.

To maintain the small lake fertility level, the manager can usually rely on visual inspection. Fertilizer is often added when it is possible to see an object at a depth of eighteen inches or more. An 8-8-2 mineral fertilizer applied at 100 pounds per surface acre should show results within three to seven days.

Unfortunately, the coloration resulting from fertilization is often interpreted by the lake user as an indication of dirty or polluted water. Therefore, for public relations purposes, the manager may be wise to consider other methods of controlling aquatic weeds.

### Chemical Control

In recent years, small lake managers have moved from the use of fertilizer to the use of chemicals for control of aquatic weed growth. Chemical control is relatively easy, and there are numerous products from which to select. In making the chemical selection, the desired environmental parameters constitute the decision-making criteria. (Table 2.2)

TABLE 2.2  *Chemical Alternatives for Controlling Aquatic Weeds*

| Problem | Materials | Application |
|---------|-----------|-------------|
| *Algae—Not Rooted* | Hydrothol Liquid or | 3 pts./surface acre |
| Planktonic (scummy or | Hydrothol Granular or | 100 lbs./surface acre 4 ft. deep |
| algae bloom) | Cutrine or | 2¼ gal./surface acre 3 ft. deep |
| Filamentous (Moss) | Copper Sulfate | 11 lbs./surface acre 4 ft. deep |
| *Algae—Rooted* | Hydrothol Granular or | 100 lbs./surface acre 4 ft. deep |
| Chara Nitella | Cutrine or | 3 gal./surface acre 3 ft. deep |
| | Copper Sulfate | 16 lbs./surface acre 4 ft. deep |
| *Submersed weeds* | | |
| Coontail | Aquathol Plus Granular or | 200 lbs./surface acre 4 ft. deep |
| Milfoil | Aquathol Plus Liquid or | 4 gal./surface acre 4 ft. deep |
| Pondweeds | Aquathol K. Granular or | 200 lbs./surface acre 4 ft. deep |
| Naiads | Aquathol K. Liquid or | 4 gal./surface acre 4 ft. deep |
| Others | Hydrothol Granular or | 100 lb./surface acre 4 ft. deep |
| | Hydrothol Liquid or | 2 gal./surface acre |
| | Diquat Liquid | 1 gal./surface acre |
| Duckweed | Diquat Liquid | 1 gal./surface acre |
| Arrowhead | Aqualthol Plus Granular or | 200 lbs./surface acre 4 ft. deep |
| Waterlily, Lotus | Aquathol Plus Liquid | 4 gal./surface acre 4 ft. deep |
| Patterdock, Watershield | | |
| Cattail, Rushes, | Dowpon and | 15 lbs./100 gal. water |
| Sedges, Sawgrass | Surfactant X-77 | 1 pint |

Oxygen depletion may occur during periods of cloudy, hot or muggy weather. It may also occur from sudden die off of phytoplankton even if no herbicide has been used or from die off of weeds after the use of herbicides. If fish gasp for air, adding one to three pounds of potassium permanganate per acre will help to satisfy the biological oxygen demand (BOD) of all plants and animals.

In applying chemicals for aquatic weed treatment, the applicator should avoid breathing fumes, dusts, or mists. Exposed skin should be washed after usage. Prior to applying chemicals, the small lake manager should check with state natural resources authorities to see if special training and/or permits are required.

## General Maintenance

With periodic routine maintenance, the small lake will provide many years of functional service. In addition to maintaining control over sedimentation, aquatic weeds, and general water quality, the small lake manager must be aware of potential problems that can develop with the dam and drain structures.

The dam and spillway should be covered with a healthy stand of grass. It should be mowed and fertilized regularly. Proper mowing helps control shrubs and weeds and results in an attractive and erosion-free structure.

Trees should not be allowed to grow on the dam or in the emergency spillway. Water from the lake can seep through the dam by following tree roots, ultimately resulting in severe leaking. Even after trees have been removed, the decaying stumps can leave holes that cause deterioration to the dam.

A trash rack on the overflow pipe, or riser, will keep floating debris from stopping up the drain structure. It also helps to keep sun off the overflow pipe (riser), giving it longer life.

# PROGRAM DEVELOPMENT

A small lake can accommodate a range of leisure programs and activities unmatched by other outdoor recreation resources of similar size. Potential activities range from those with which we are most familiar (e.g., boating, fishing, and swimming) to environmentally oriented educational programs. The small lake also provides an excellent natural feature for recreation activities not directly dependent upon the availability of water. Picnic areas adjacent to a small lake, for example, will nearly always attract more users than similar areas lacking a water feature.

Public agencies, as well as privately owned recreation businesses, have long known of the nature of small lakes to provide a wide range of recreation activities and to attract large numbers of people. As a result, the small lake is often viewed as a revenue-producing complex that, when planned and managed properly, should be able to generate significant financial resources. If fiscal self-sufficiency is a goal, it is important to identify those program areas that have revenue potential. In addition, it is vital that the manager is familiar with the types of equipment and facilities that will attract users and will hold up under the pressure of heavy use.

## Boating

Boating has the greatest revenue production potential of the water-based activities at a pond or small lake. In selecting watercraft for rental purposes, it is important to know the types of boats that will attract users. Once the type, or types, of watercraft have been identified, it is important to apply several selection criteria to the numerous boats available for purchase to assure many years of safe usage. The following considerations should be examined in selecting boats for a rental operation:

*1. Popularity.* For the most part, the boating activity at a small lake will be for recreational purposes rather than as a conveyance for anglers. However, in situations where the pond or small lake is a popular fishing area, and where the lake is of a size and shape where bank fishing leads to limited success, it may be wise to provide fishing boats. The angler's primary concern is for a boat that is convenient for fishing rather than aesthetics. Rental boat selection considerations should focus on criteria dealing with maintenance, durability, and safety.

The selection of watercraft to meet the needs of the recreational boater is more complex due to the many products available and to the fact that most rentals will be impulsive rather than planned. As a result, the watercraft must attract the attention of the potential user.

The small lake manager should not underestimate the influence of children in determining the ultimate success of boat rental operation. Parents and grandparents are vulnerable to boating activities that attract the interest of children. Parents and grandparents are interested in activities where they can participate with their children. As a result, it is important to select watercraft that appear to be fun and exciting. The popularity of pedal boats as rental craft reflects the attempt to attract the interest of children. The 1961 *Manual and Survey on Small Lake Management* provides advice relative to the selection of rental craft that is still sound:

> Rowboats may appeal to the older age groups while youngsters and the more adventurous are likely to favor the watercycle or paddle boat. A craft that is unusual and can accommodate a family, with the youngsters supplying the power, is the answer for parents of determined children. Thus, a boat designed for double occupancy with enough room to safely accommodate one or two young sailors is by far the most popular craft. As these boats are usually rented for a higher fee, the arrangement works out to the management's advantage.[8]

Today, there are a number of recreation products and watercrafts that have been designed to appeal to the youthful spirit in all visitors. Sailboards, motorized surfboards, water tricycles, slides, and cable waterskiing are just a few. While there is no doubt that they appear to be exciting, many are very expensive, and require large areas of open water and careful maintenance.

*2. Safety.* Most boats on the market today are safe for normal boating and have a considerable margin to minimize the danger of overloading. In spite of the inherent stability of most boats, accidents can occur. A certain amount of horseplay is to be expected. Close supervision and strict rule enforcement are necessary to minimize the danger of capsizing, falling from rental craft, or other accidents that can result in equipment damage, injuries, or drownings. Examples of boating rules that might be utilized are as follows:

- Boaters must stay seated.
- Avoid hitting other boats or structures.
- Do not run boats aground.
- Do not transfer to other boats.
- Do not splash or disturb other boaters.
- Keep reasonable distance from other boaters, fishermen, and other lake users.
- Boats must return promptly to dock when called.

Rules governing rental craft use should be clearly posted at the boathouse and on each boat. They should be brief and easy to read. Rule violators should be dealt with immediately to avoid further violations and to minimize any inconvenience to other visitors.

Federal law requires that all boaters have with them a U.S. Coast Guard approved personal flotation device (PFD). While the law does not require that the boater wear the PFD, it is a good policy to have young children do so. Boat attendants should be sure the lifejacket fits and is adjusted properly.

A safety boat equipped with an outboard motor should be readily available in case of emergency. The boat should be equipped with throwable life rings and reaching poles. Life rings with fifty to seventy-five feet of one-fourth-inch diameter rope should also be placed around the perimeter of the lake. Such measures not only help assure the safety of visitors, but could also minimize liability insurance premiums.

*3. Maintenance.* Most boats are built to provide years of service under normal use. However, many watercraft are designed for personal use rather than as rental equipment. As a result, special care should be taken to select watercraft that are well constructed, but that can be quickly repaired and placed back into service.

The most common materials found in rowboats, canoes, and pedal boats are aluminum and fiberglass. Heat-treated or aircraft grade aluminum boats are particularly durable and many times stronger than boats made of standard aluminum. Seams should be sealed and riveted. Generally speaking, a boat seam with closely spaced rivets will be stronger, and will result in fewer leaks, than those with rivets spaced every two to three inches. Heat-treated aluminum boats have been known to provide many years of low maintenance service as rental craft. Occasionally, however, punctures will occur requiring a special welding process (heliarc). Welding services are usually available locally. Tanglewood Park in Clemmons, North Carolina, uses a local technical college for aluminum welding services. Welding costs are minimized while students are provided with a good learning experience.

Fiberglass boats are attractive as well as strong. Boat corners and edges may crack and break as a result of unnecessary bumping into docks or other boats. Major repairs may keep the boat out of operation for several days and require skilled workmanship to match the original gel-coat surface. Fiberglass repairs made by less skilled individuals may be as strong as new but usually look patched and discolored.

Some canoes and other small watercrafts are made of plastic-type materials. While they are strong and colorful, they are difficult to repair.

As watercraft become more complex, the degree of maintenance required to keep them in operation increases. Watercraft with moving parts will require more maintenance than those without. Similarly, watercraft with engines or motors will require frequent routine maintenance as well as emergency repairs to keep them in operation. Most small lake operations avoid renting equipment that depends upon engines or electric motors for propulsion. Such crafts are usually very expensive and require highly skilled repair persons to keep them in operation. It is good practice to stock those parts that break down most often to assure quick repair and reentry into the rental fleet.

Other factors to be considered in selecting rental craft are initial cost, number of occupants, and revenue generation potential. Table 2.3 may be of value in comparing selected rental craft as to their relative strengths and weaknesses.

*Boat rentals.* For many years, the standard of five boats per acre was recommended for small lake rental operations. That guideline still results in a safe and pleasant boating environment with plenty of room for the novice to avoid collisions. There are, however, some examples of small lake operations where the ratio of pedal boats per acre of water surface is as high as ten to one with no apparent negative problems. In situations where more than one type of boat is being rented (e.g., pedal boats and rowboats), the ratio of five to one should be observed.

To insure a smooth boating program and the maximum use of all boats, an efficient system for renting and recalling boats must be established. One method is to fill out an application when the boat is rented, noting information that is important for control and record keeping. The receipt is given to the boater who then has a record of the boat number, time of leaving, time due back, and the charge made. The boater need only show the receipt to the dock attendant at the indicated time to receive the assigned boat. Boats are called in by number over a public address system when the time is up. This system is particularly effective on busy days.

In those cases where the number of boats exceeds the demand, the boats may not be recalled. Instead, the boaters pay the fee for the minimum time period prior to taking the boat and pay for any time over that, on a prorated basis, upon returning.

An efficient rental operation may have each boat rented as many as twenty times per day, assuming the rental period is a half-hour. A number of small lake operations rent pedal boats on a twenty-minute basis, especially on weekends and holidays when there is great demand for anything that floats. That may seem to be a very short time period, but it is usually long enough to tire out the typical boater while adding one rental period per hour per boat.

TABLE 2.3  *Rental Craft Selection Criteria*

| Type of Watercraft | Popularity | Accident Incidence | Initial Cost | Maintenance Requirements | Repair Difficulty | Skill Requirement | Capacity | Comments |
|---|---|---|---|---|---|---|---|---|
| Pedal Boat | VH | L | H | H | M–H | VL | 2–4 | Repair parts should be stocked. |
| Rowboats | M | VL | L | VL | L | M | 3–4 | Pointed bow more popular than flat bow or Jon boat for pleasure. No difference as fishing boat. |
| Canoe | H | M | L | VL | L | L–M | 2 | Select flat bottom design. |
| Kayak-type craft | H | M | L | VL | L | L | 1 | Best location adjacent to swimming area due to frequency of boater getting wet. |
| Motorboat | VH | H | VH | VH | VH | L | 3–4 | Keeping motors in running order a major problem. |
| Wind-surfboard | VH | M–H | H | H | M | VH | 1 | Requires instructor. |
| Sailboat (board type) | VH | M | VH | H | H | H | 2 | Requires instructor. |

Key: VH, Very High; H, High; M, Medium or Average; L, Low; VL, Very Low.

Boat liveries usually require a deposit equal to four or five hours of rental, and the customer gets a refund or pays the balance upon returning. Fishing boats are usually available at an optional daily rate that is somewhat less than the regular hourly rate charged for pleasure boats for an entire day. Anchors should be provided with fishing boats at no extra charge.

*Competition between boats and fishing.*  Where there are multiple uses of a limited resource, it is inevitable that conflict will eventually arise. A small lake that offers pleasure boating and fishing is no exception. Many anglers interpret the thrashing of oars and paddles, or pedal boats crossing fishing lines as intentional harassment. Likewise, an errant angler's cast that comes close to striking the pleasure boater is often thought to have been intentional. In most cases, however, it is limited boating or fishing skill, or the common use of the same small lake area by diverse recreators that causes misunderstanding. It may be wise to consider zoning an area strictly for fishing so the angler can enjoy his activity in solitude and boaters can avoid worrying about flying hooks and sinkers.

As far as any negative effects from boating disturbance, it has been proven on numerous occasions that boats, even motorboats, do not result in water quality degradation or poor fishing. Because the wave action from large boats may cause some bank erosion, they are usually prohibited from smaller lakes. There is no denying, however, that it is disconcerting for the angler to lose lures and yards of fishing line to pedal boats propelled by oblivious boaters.

Zoning about one third of the lake exclusively for fishing usually results in a compatible situation. On days of light use, boating and fishing can coexist. On days of heavy use, the anglers will naturally gravitate to the solitude of the area zoned exclusively for fishing.

Areas zoned for fishing should have some overhanging trees and shrubs. Fish will be attracted to these areas to avoid the heat of the sun and to forage for worms and insects that fall from the vegetation into the water.

## Fishing

Fishing is one of the most popular outdoor recreation activities in North America. Fishing transcends socioeconomic levels in that it can be just as enjoyable to the cane pole and worm angler as it is to the deep sea troller. Because of the high demand for fishing waters, many anglers are attracted to local ponds and small lakes. The peaceful environment of small impoundments makes them excellent for family outings and for teaching children basic fishing skills. In addition, some of the biggest "lunker" bass have been caught in ponds and small lakes.

The small lake manager is faced with a perplexing problem in deciding what type of fishing program to provide. The options range from nonmanagement, in which case the fish population will usually become dominated by stunted blue gill or bream, to the provision of a fee fishing lake requiring intensive management to assure successful fishing.

To better understand the fishing program options available to the manager, it is necessary to be familiar with the carrying capacity of small lakes. The naturally productive small lake may support 150 to 200 pounds of fish per surface acre of water. The ideal situation would be to have a balance of game fish, such as bass, blue gill, and catfish, with a good mix in size. Theoretically, the fish population could be made up of 100 two-pound fish or perhaps 1,600 two-ounce fish. While neither situation would normally exist, it is obvious that a large population of stunted fish would not attract the serious angler. Nor would it be wise to charge a fishing fee.

The question, then, is whether the lake's potential is being realized by accommodating a small number of anglers or a children's program needing little management, or whether an intensive program is to be provided that will attract large numbers of serious anglers expecting to catch their limit of "keepers." In either case, it is important to get the advice of a fisheries biologist. Such assistance is available from state fish and wildlife offices.

Fish ponds or small lakes are classified as warm-water or cold-water. The typical warm-water lake is principally intended for bass, bluegill (or bream), and catfish, while the cold-water fishery is generally intended for trout. The kind of fish stocked in a pond will depend on geographic location, size of the impoundment, and the kind of fish likely to be popular among users of the lake. Geographic location is the principal consideration; trout ponds, for example, are most likely to succeed in northern temperate areas of the country but may succeed in other areas if fed by cold springs.[9]

Maintaining a balanced game fish population is a challenge even for the experts. It may be necessary to eliminate all existing species from time to time in order to restock with a balanced fish population. The Soil Conservation Service and State Fish and Wildlife Offices will usually advise on the stocking and management of fisheries that will be open at no charge to the general public.

*Fee fishing.* An alternative for the small lake fishing program is the establishment of a fee-fishing program, where the angler either pays for the right to fish or pays for any fish caught. Most fee-fishing lakes are privately operated as small businesses. However, it is an option public park and recreation agencies may want to consider. If natural water resources are productive and easily reached, the need for fee fishing may be small. However, if public fishing water is scarce and if there are large numbers of people in close proximity, a fee-fishing lake might provide an excellent recreation resource for anglers that lack the time or money to travel to far removed natural fishing waters. Fee-fishing lakes are particularly popular in highly populated metropolitan areas and tourist areas.

In most cases, the angler is charged a fee for the right to fish and is charged an additional fee for each fish kept. Guidelines to consider in establishing a fee-fishing lake are as follows:

1. A permit fee is usually charged for the right to fish. The angler should be provided with a badge or permit that can be observed by lake management personnel. Children may not be charged a permit fee but should pay the standard fee for all fish kept.
2. Uninjured fish may be released, but anglers should be discouraged from returning bleeding or injured fish to the water. Once a fish is placed on a stringer, it should not be returned to the water.
3. Anglers can be charged by length for any fish kept. Fees for larger fish should be higher than those for small fish; fees for prized game fish (e.g., trout and bass), should be higher than those for catfish and other less sought-after species.
4. The use of live minnows should be prohibited. Those that get free of hooks, or are discarded by anglers at the end of the day, can propogate and take over the lake, thus destroying it as a fee-fishing operation.
5. Anglers should be limited to the use of one fishing pole at a time.
6. Anglers should be encouraged to use barbless hooks. Attendants should offer to snip the barb off hooks for all users.

Prior to establishing a fee-fishing operation, state conservation agencies should be contacted to determine requirements for operator and/or user license fees. The potential success of fee-fishing lakes is greater in states that do not require users to have a fishing license. This is of particular significance to park operations and in tourist areas where a high percentage of business is likely to be with transient or casual anglers who do not generally purchase licenses.

Rental fishing rods might be made available for the transient or impulse angler. While they will not generate a significant amount of revenue, they should more than pay for themselves over the course of a single season. Cane poles will usually prove to be satisfactory for the novice or for children while spincast outfits are excellent for the older or more experienced angler.

## Swimming

Swimming is the most popular outdoor recreation activity of U.S. citizens. As such, it is nearly impossible for public park and recreation agencies to keep up with the demand for pools and beaches. In cases where the demand for swimming is high, facilities are inadequate, and good fishing water is abundant elsewhere, it may be wise to consider a swimming area as part of the small lake operation.

Lakes of just a few acres usually cannot accommodate both fishing and swimming. Local health departments may require that the swimming area be chlorinated. Chlorination of small lake swimming areas is possible but would result in the eventual death of the entire fish population. If a lake is located on a stream, or is spring fed to the point where adequate water quality can be maintained without the addition of chlorine, swimming and fishing can exist compatibly. Otherwise, a choice between the two must be made. Chapter 5 provides guidelines for the planning, construction, and management of beaches.

## Educational Programs

The small lake can be an excellent resource for educational programs that can be beneficial to both the participant and the recreation agency or business. Educational programs might fall into one of two classifications: (1) environmental education or (2) outdoor recreation skills education.

Environmental education programs emphasize knowledge of the natural environment. Such programs might be provided by the lake staff, park naturalist, school teachers, or volunteers. The small lake can be an excellent field laboratory for the study of aquatic ecology, plants, and wildlife, as well as basic conservation concepts and practices. The small lake environmental education program might be the primary focus of a youth nature club, such as the junior naturalists, or one segment of a day camp or nature center program.

Small lakes can also be utilized for outdoor recreation skills instruction. The relative protection from wind and waves makes the small lake an ideal instructional facility for canoeing, rowing, and casting. Even windsurfing and sailing, while more enjoyable on larger water bodies by skilled users, are more easily learned on small lakes.

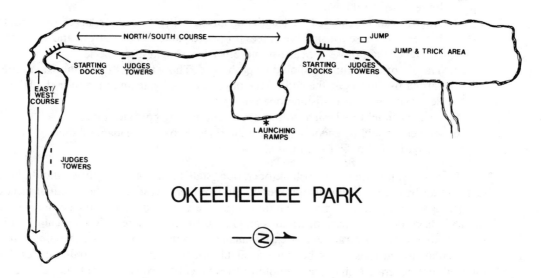

**FIGURE 2.5** *Okeeheelee Park Lake in Palm Beach County Florida was constructed specifically for water skiing.* Having two perpendicular courses guarantees protection from wind.

*Source:* Palm Beach County Florida Department of Parks and Recreation.

Most communities have clubs oriented towards boating, fishing, conservation, and environmental protection. In many cases the special interest groups that have been permitted to use the small lake facilities for meetings and other programs have reciprocated with fish stockings, sponsorship of special events, and in making physical improvements that will benefit all users.

Small lake and other resource managers who ignore educational programs are not only missing an excellent public relations opportunity but are underestimating the values that can be realized through those efforts. There are three important benefits from educational programs:

1. *Resource protection.* The small lake is an extremely fragile ecosystem. Educational programs can result in a more knowledgeable user which can lead to fewer incidents of misuse. The proper use of boats and other recreation equipment, promoted through skills instructional programs, will result in less equipment damage. As a result, the equipment will maintain its appearance longer and will not have to be replaced as often.

2. *User safety.* The boater or angler that has completed a sound instructional program is almost assured of fewer injuries from that activity. Knowledge of the proper use of

equipment will result in fewer accidents to users and spectators alike. It should be remembered that a minor boating mishap can result in a tragic accident.

3. *Maximum enjoyment.* Most people derive the most pleasure from those activities in which they do well. The development of boating and fishing skills will enable the participants to maximize their enjoyment from the activity. The canoeist that can manuever that craft at will has the opportunity to explore the beauty of quiet coves and inlets while the unskilled boater thrashes out of control, often causing others to compromise their enjoyment.

## PERSONNEL

Most small lakes are staffed primarily by seasonal employees who have only a minor investment in the ultimate success or failure of the operation. And yet, it is the actions of the manager, dock attendants, instructors, and fee collectors that will determine the efficiency and personality of the small lake environment.

The supervisory, public relations, programming, environmental control, and fiscal management responsibilities require a great deal from the small lake manager. The training of a full-time manager should be in outdoor or natural resources recreation management. The manager should possess skills, knowledge, and interests in a wide range of related areas. Such a person lends authority and may serve as a resource consultant on lake, fish management, and conservation matters for the entire community.

In addition to the usual duties, the manager must be able to sell the facility and concepts of recreation and conservation through knowledge, competence, and enthusiasm. The manager might organize casting and fly tying classes, instruct boating courses, conduct nature walks, speak on conservation subjects to civic and outdoor groups, and appear on television or radio. All these activities enhance the stature of the lake program.

Dock attendants and fee collectors should be neat, uniformed, personable, and responsible individuals who will create a positive impression for the lake through their courteous assistance. The uniform, which may consist of a standardized shirt with the park logo and name, is an important aid to visitors in identifying persons of authority. Rubber-soled shoes, preferably deck shoes, should be worn by all dock attendants to avoid slipping on wet docks and boats.

The entire staff should be expected to accept responsibility for the cleanliness and appearance of the facility. A well-maintained recreation complex is appreciated by most visitors and develops a sense of pride in the staff.

The manager and dock attendants should have completed appropriate training programs through the American Red Cross or other recognized organizations. The courses are available at central locations throughout the United States and emphasize aquatic skills and instructional techniques. The training will prove to be of value even to experienced boaters.

## SUMMARY

The purpose of this chapter has been to discuss considerations for the planning, construction, and management of small lakes for recreation. Water is a magnet for attracting people. The smallest pond in a public area will draw children and adults seeking the unique activities and respite that water provides. Few projects can offer the wide appeal and intensive use for a moderate expenditure as can a small lake. If planned, constructed, and managed properly, a small lake offers more diversity of activities for its size than any other park facility and should be capable of generating revenue in excess of operating costs. With current emphasis on revenue production and fiscal management, consideration should be given to the development of lake areas as part of the total recreation system. In conclusion, the small lake has the potential of becoming an extremely popular recreation resource capable of attracting thousands of participants while avoiding any cost to the taxpayer.

## NOTES

1. Hall, Norvill L., *Manual and Survey on Small Lake Management,* Management Aid No. 8 National Recreation and Park Association, Alexandria, Va., 1961, p. 8.

2. Tourbier, Joachim, *Lakes and Ponds,* Technical Bulletin No. 72, The Urban Land Institute, Washington, D.C., 1976.

3. U.S. Department of Agriculture, *Ponds for Water Supply and Recreation,* Agriculture Handbook No. 387, Soil Conservation Service (Washington, D.C., January, 1971), p. 27.

4. The Urban Land Institute, "Lakes and Ponds," p. 4.

5. *Ibid.,* p. 17.

6. Hall, *Manual and Survey,* p. 10.

7. U.S. Department of Agriculture, *Warm-Water Fishponds,* Farmers Bulletin No. 2250, Washington, D.C., 1977, p. 10.

8. Hall, *Manual and Survey,* p. 13.

9. The Urban Land Institute, "Lakes and Ponds," p. 32.

# 3

# LARGE LAKE MANAGEMENT

We are fortunate in the United States to have excellent large lakes available for recreation. These natural resources are more plentiful in some sections of the country than others. However, most Americans live within a reasonable driving distance of a relatively large lake. Most of our approximately 100,000 natural lakes are located in the Northeast and northern Midwest. In addition, there are thousands of man-made lakes. (The term *reservoir* is often used to distinguish a man-made lake from a natural lake. In this chapter, we will not make such a distinction, but rather will use the term *lake* for both man-made and natural inland bodies of standing water.) These lakes have tremendous recreation potential. The lake surface itself provides opportunities for swimming, boating, and fishing. The lake environment is a pleasant

PHOTO 3.1 *Large lakes provide opportunities for a wide variety of recreational activity.*

place for people to spend some of their leisure hours, and it enhances such onshore activities as picnicking, camping, hiking, and observing wildlife.

For purposes of this chapter we are defining a *large lake* as being approximately 500 acres or more. This standard is used because lake managers generally agree that it takes a lake of this size to accommodate a complete mix of boating activity; that is, power boating, waterskiing, sailing, and fishing. There are certainly factors that would make a particular 350 or 400-acre lake usable for this mix of activity. Conversely, there are 1000-acre lakes where the mix of activity cannot reasonably take place. The factors that influence recreation use on a lake will be discussed later.

Recreation use is rarely the primary reason a large lake is constructed. Large, man-made lakes are generally built for one of the following reasons: (1) electric power (either hydroelectric or for cooling coal or nuclear-powered steam plants), (2) flood control, (3) domestic water supply, (4) irrigating agricultural crops. It is not unusual for a lake to be constructed for multiple purposes (e.g., flood control and domestic water supply). In recent years recreation use has become a more and more important justification for construction of large lakes.

## MANAGING AGENCIES

As there are a variety of reasons for large lakes being constructed in the United States, there are also a variety of managing agencies that own or control the water surface and/or shoreline. Large lakes are managed by the following agencies: (1) federal government, (2) state parks, (3) utility companies, (4) local government agencies, (5) private industry, and (6) private individuals.

### Federal Government

*U.S. Army Corps of Engineers.*   With more than 400 lakes and 10 million acres of land and water surface, the Corps manages probably the largest water-oriented recreation program in the United States. Their involvement dates back to the Flood Control Act of 1944 which provided the first clear federal policy concerning recreation uses of water resource projects. The Corps was authorized to construct, operate, and maintain public recreation facilities. The Federal Water Projects Act of 1965 (Public Law 89–72) gave recreation equal billing with other uses. This act states that up to 50 percent of the benefits of a lake can be for recreation.

*Bureau of Reclamation.*   Operating in seventeen western states, this agency has been primarily involved in developing lakes for electric power and agricultural irrigation. It has been their policy to turn over recreation operations to other federal, state, or local agencies.

*Tennessee Valley Authority.*   Located in seven southeastern states, TVA was created for flood control, navigation, and electric power on the Tennessee River. Other than their recreation demonstration area, Land Between the Lakes, they generally do not operate recreation facilities, but rather make land available to other public agencies and private groups for development and management.

*Fish and Wildlife Service.*   Recreation is viewed as an appropriate secondary purpose on national wildlife refuges. Lakes managed by the Bureau of Sport Fisheries and Wildlife do not generally encourage a mix of recreational activities, but rather emphasize those activities that are more appropriate for wildlife refuges; namely, hunting, fishing, and wildlife observation.

### State Parks

State parks and state recreation areas have been developed around many natural and man-made lakes. In some instances states have jurisdiction over the water surface of natural lakes but have no shoreline control, creating serious management problems.

## Utility Companies

Since a large number of lakes in the United States have been developed for hydroelectric power or as cooling lakes for steam generating plants, utility companies control lakes with great recreation potential. Involvement of public utility companies in providing lands for recreation can be traced to the creation of the Federal Energy Commission. In 1920 the Federal Power Act created the Federal Energy Commission and provided that all license applications for hydroelectric power projects be accompanied by a "comprehensive scheme of improvement and utilization for the purposes of navigation, water-power development, and *other beneficial uses.*" Amendments to the Federal Power Act of 1935 specifically named recreation as an "other beneficial use." In 1963 the Federal Energy Commission further strengthened the act when they passed a regulation that required all applications for major licenses to be accompanied by a recreation plan. After some confusion on the part of the applicants concerning what a recreation plan should contain, the Federal Energy Commission (renamed the Federal Energy Regulatory Commission in 1977) reworded the code. The regulation, as amended in 1965, requires that all recreation plans include the following:

- A map showing the location of all project lands depicting those areas that are to be preserved by the licensee for existing or proposed recreation use.
- The location of existing and proposed recreation facilities including boat launching ramps, picnicking and camping facilities, access roads, trails, and the provision for sanitary facilities and waste disposal.
- A statement of which facilities the licensee plans to provide at its own cost or in cooperation with others.
- Estimate of public recreation use of the project.
- A statement of the extent of consultation and cooperation with appropriate federal, state, and local recreation authorities and copies of all such agreements.

Some utility companies had been providing for the recreation use of their properties long before the Federal Energy Regulatory Commission made it mandatory. An example of this is Lake Wallenpaupack, owned by the Pennsylvania Power and Light Company. Recreation facilities have been provided along this thirteen-mile lake since 1926. Another example is Merwin Park in southeastern Washington. This park along the Merwin Dam was opened for public use in 1934 by the Pacific Power and Light Company.

## Local Government Agencies

Many lakes that were constructed primarily for use as domestic water supply, are owned by a municipality, town, or county. These lakes are generally located either within the city limits or at least very close to the city, making them accessible to large population groups. Many of these lakes are extensively developed for recreation use and are heavily used. It is not unusual for a major city park to be built on the shoreline of one of these lakes.

## Private Industry

Industries requiring large amounts of power (e.g., aluminum), have constructed their own lakes and use the hydroelectric or steam power to operate their plants.

## Private Individuals

Some large natural and man-made lakes are owned by individuals who may choose to keep them for private, exclusive recreation use or who may open them to public use, sometimes with a profit-making motive.

## Factors Affecting Recreation on Lakes

Ownership and major purpose for development, in the case of man-made lakes, may have an enormous effect upon the way the lake is managed for recreation use. There are also other physical and locational factors that can greatly affect the types of recreation that can be carried out at a particular lake. Some of these factors include:

1. *Geographic.* Location of the lake in relation to user population can influence its use. There are a number of beautiful lakes in western North Carolina and eastern Tennessee that are so remote in their location that recreation use will never be very heavy. Conversely, Lake Hartwell in South Carolina is seventy-five miles from Altanta and yet receives considerable regular use by people living in the Atlanta area because of good interstate highway access.
2. *Topography.* There are many mountain lakes where the shoreline surrounding the lake is so steep that lakeshore development is impractical.
3. *Water Depth.* In flat, coastal areas large lakes with very shallow water depth can be found. These lakes may be excellent for fishing and small craft activity but are unusable by sail or power boats.
4. *Shoreline Configuration.* The shape of the lake may be a limiting factor. A 1000-acre lake extending in many directions with very narrow fingers may also be unusable for power boating or sailing activity.
5. *Pollution.* This can also make a lake unusable for recreation. Fortunately, some progress has been made in correcting this problem. The Federal Water Pollution Control Act of 1972 gives special attention to the quality of water in lakes as part of achieving national clean water goals. The act requires each state to:
   • Identify and classify according to eutrophic condition all publicly owned freshwater lakes within the state.
   • Prepare procedures, processes, and methods, including land use requirements, to control pollution of lakes.
   • Develop methods and procedures to restore the quality of lakes.

Even when all the physical contingencies are considered, the single most important factor concerning the quantity and quality of recreation opportunities on large lakes is management. The manner in which lakes are managed does indeed make a difference and will be the concern in the rest of this chapter. Issues related to the management of large lakes will be addressed. Each of these issues is important and must be considered by the successful lake manager.

## GOALS, OBJECTIVES, AND MANAGEMENT PHILOSOPHY

An agency's goals or management philosophy form the foundation upon which operating policies for recreation are formulated. These goals must be based upon sound principles of recreation management. In an age of changing technology and social values, it is imperative that the agency adopt a dynamic philosophy. Concise and realizable objectives also must be formulated to chart the course by which the agency's goals can be achieved. Well-defined goals and objectives provide a policy framework, a backbone, for all recreation operations.

Goals and objectives should be formulated through a regional planning effort. In various regions of the country, there are clusters of lakes, and their management can best be affected by planning recreation use on a regional basis. In all instances goals and objectives should be oriented to achieve maximum public benefits. They should be documented in written form to provide a policy framework for recreation operations. They should be thoroughly understood by all agency employees. The goals and objectives should not be written one time and then forgotten. Rather, they should be dynamic and flexible to allow for changing conditions. They should be periodically reviewed and revised when necessary.

Because of the wide variety of agencies managing large lakes and because large lakes quite frequently cross political boundaries (city, county, and state lines), jurisdictional responsibility often becomes a problem. Ideally large lakes should be managed in the following manner:

- Lakes under federal jurisdiction should be developed and managed using all available resources of the region including the resources of state and local government and private enterprise.
- Natural lakes should be managed by the state.
- Municipal lakes should be managed by a municipal or county park and recreation department.
- Lakes under private ownership (e.g., a utility company or industry) may be managed in several acceptable ways including self-management or delegating management to government agencies and/or private enterprise under local controls. However, one of the best ways is to assign jurisdictional responsibility to a lake authority under governmental auspices with total responsibility for lake development and operation, with the private entity retaining only enough control to ensure noninterference with their private operations.

## SHORELINE CONTROL AND DEVELOPMENT

Recreation opportunities for lake users depend upon policies related to shoreline control and development. The agency must be concerned with those onshore and offshore developments which give public or private access to the lake surface, developed because of the esthetic value provided by the lake, and which originate on the lakeshore and project onto or under the lake surface, or as floating structures adjacent to but not directly connected to the shore. A sound development plan for the lake shoreline is essential to ensure the accomplishment of the agency's goals and objectives.

One of the first steps that must be taken is to define the term *shoreline*. Shoreline can legitimately be defined as the "flood pool level," the "normal pool," or the "average drawdown level for the past ten years." There are instances when each of the above definitions ought to apply to the term *shoreline*. Shoreline regulations have very little meaning if shoreline is not clearly defined in those regulations.

It is essential that the managing agency have and maintain control of the entire lake shoreline. This is necessary to assure control of shoreline development as well as control of activity on the water surface. This does not preclude second and third-party agreements consistent with recreation objectives.

A desirable method of developing public facilities on lakes under private jurisdiction is to encourage government agencies to develop the lake shoreline by granting leases at no cost to the agency or by land transfer to these agencies. Agencies should use extreme caution in allowing private cottage development. Private cottage development should be permitted only when adequate and appropriate public access to the lake is ensured by access zones, rights of way, developed sites, and sites reserved for future development. When an agency allows structures (e.g., piers and boathouses) to be built, it should control these structures by issuing a permit only after plans for these structures have been submitted to the agency for approval. This is important for esthetic and safety control. Dredging or changes in shoreline contour should not be allowed. Violation of this principle can lead to severe environmental damage to the lake shoreline both physically and esthetically. All lease agreements permitting development of recreation facilities should be written and should contain a reversionary clause stating that the property reverts to the owner if land is not used as proposed. Shoreline development regulations should be enforced by the operating agency with a minimum of two on-site visits per year.

## PROTECTION AND PRESERVATION
## OF SHORELINE ENVIRONMENT

The esthetic qualities of a lake have wide public appeal. Many persons derive pleasure from the beauty of a lake and its surroundings without venturing onto the lake surface itself. Every effort should be made to retain the natural appearance of the lakeshore. Developed areas and facilities should blend with the environment rather than protrude from it.

The managing agency should make a land-use study and encourage governmental units surrounding the lake to adopt a zoning ordinance(s). As a part of the zoning ordinance, the agency should establish areas that are not to be developed for intensive recreation use. Agencies should preserve scenic areas surrounding the lake, particularly those seen from a highway, by allowing no timber cutting in these areas. There is a need to protect areas particularly subject to erosion from wave action through the use of riprap, wooden pilings, or other artificial means.

The agency should enter into the following kinds of cooperative agreements with:

- The state wildlife agency to stock the lake with fish and manage other wildlife areas.
- Farmers to cooperatively farm agency land. One lake allows farmers to farm agency land, harvest 75 percent of the crop, and leave 25 percent in the field for wildlife.
- Private land owners in the immediate lake area and in the lake watershed to help prevent soil erosion.

Finally, the managing agency should prohibit recreation use of areas that will endanger wildlife (e.g., spawning beds and wildlife banding areas).

# DRAWDOWN

Although drawdown is not a problem for recreation users on all lakes, it is a persistent one on many reservoirs and impoundments. We have already discussed the fact that the primary reason for the existence of many large lakes is flood control, power development, and water supply or irrigation. The conflict between primary use resulting in significant or severe drawdown and recreation use is obvious. The importance of recreation use of lakes is becoming more widely recognized, and the lake on which drawdown can be controlled during the recreation season becomes a much more valuable recreation resource. With this in mind, the agency should limit drawdown to a level acceptable to the recreation user during the recreation season.

# RECORDS OF RECREATIONAL LAKE USE

Accurate records of recreational lake use provide a valuable tool for the lake manager for use in reports to the governing authority, for budget purposes, to help determine lake capacity for recreation use, and to help in planning new facilities. Variables such as lake size, shoreline configuration, and access points dictate the use of varying methods and techniques to determine recreation use.

If access to the lake is controlled, daily records of use should be kept. On lakes with multiple, uncontrolled access points, use should be estimated through the use of traffic counters supplemented by on-site surveys. Records should include where users come from and the length of time the user spends *at* the lake and *on* the lake.

# WATER SURFACE ZONING

In addition to a master land-use plan for a lake, agencies should develop a master water-use plan coordinated with the land-use plan. Such a plan should be established for all lakes, regardless of size and amount of use. Water surface zoning methods such as area zoning, time zoning, and protective space zoning can be used effectively to separate incompatible activities. For any zoning method to be effective, the agency must enforce and seek public support for established water surface zoning regulations.

The three possible methods of zoning water surface activities are described as follows:

1. *Area zoning.* Different sections (areas) of the lake are zoned for different activities. For example, one section of the lake may be reserved for sailing or arms of a lake may be zoned for fishing, and all boats entering the areas must do so at no-wake speed. Area zoning is very practical and widely used.
2. *Time zoning.* A lake or sections of a lake are designated for different activities at different times of the day or days of the week. For example, waterskiing could be allowed each day from noon to 5:00 P.M., or the lake could be designated for sailing only on Thursdays. This method of zoning also works well, but it requires careful communication with lake users. The power boat operator who comes to the lake on Thursday only to find the lake is closed to him will not be very happy.
3. *Protective space zoning.* This type of zoning is dynamic. Boats must maintain a certain distance (e.g., 100 feet) from each other as they move on the lake. This type of zoning is not frequently used because (1) people's perception of distance on the open water is not reliable, and (2) it is difficult to enforce.

Regardless of whether the entire lake water surface is zoned or not, and regardless of the method of zoning that is utilized, the following minimal zoning regulations should be established:

1. Designate no-wake zones in all danger areas such as around launching ramps and swimming areas.
2. Designate areas for fishing and allow other boats to enter these areas only at no-wake speed.
3. Restrict all recreation activities in an area near the dam of man-made lakes. The recommended distance is 1,500 feet.

## GENERAL REGULATION OF RECREATION LAKE USE

Certain general regulations regarding recreation lake use are necessary; however, care must be taken not to overregulate. The best regulation is no regulation unless it (1) protects the public, (2) is fully enforced, and (3) is nondiscriminatory. The desirability of many general lake regulations depends upon local conditions and the local use patterns. General lake regulations should inlude the following:

1. The state should require that all boats (or at least motorboats over 10 horsepower) be registered.
2. Prohibit operating boat while intoxicated.
3. Prohibit littering shoreline or lake surface.
4. Prohibit camping and picnicking at other than developed, designated areas.

## HEALTH REGULATIONS AND HEALTH MANAGEMENT PRACTICES

Health regulations and health management practices should be formulated and enforced cooperatively by state and local authorities and the lake managing authority. There should be no compromise in the use of shorelands or of the lake surface with regard to public health and sanitation.

State and/or local health departments should:

1. Carry out inspections of water supplies, sewage treatment systems, and general sanitation of camping areas, picnic areas, and other facilities.

2. Regulate against boats dumping sewage into the water. Boats that are equipped with marine toilets also should be equipped with a holding tank or sewage treatment device that has been approved by the state health department, or should have all discharge fittings sealed.
3. Monitor recreation use of lakes built as primary or secondary water supplies. (Swimming should be allowed in lakes serving as primary or secondary water supplies only when treatment facilities are adequate to ensure a safe public water supply.)

The operating agency should control:

1. Water quality in swimming areas by testing regularly for conditions that may be harmful to swimmers.
2. Pollution in the lake from any source and seek help of local stream pollution control boards to clear up the source of such pollution.
3. Prohibit use of lake property for toilet purposes other than at standard sanitary facilities. On lakes that serve as primary or secondary water supplies, all boats should be equipped with containers to be used for sanitary purposes only.

## SAFETY REGULATIONS

In addition to public health and sanitation, a concern for public safety is vital to good lake management. The agency must make every effort to remove hazardous conditions that might endanger the safety of users. An effort also must be made to establish regulations that do not discriminate against a particular type of legitimate recreation activity.

### Establishing Carrying Capacities

One of the first considerations should be to limit the use of a lake to the number of boats or other watercraft which can safely use the area—to establish a carrying capacity for the lake. A management goal should be to determine the optimal recreation carrying capacity for a lake. Optimum recreation carrying capacity is defined as the amount of recreation use which reflects the level of use most appropriate for both the protection of the resource and the satisfaction of the participant. This concept involves two major elements:

1. *Physical carrying capacity*—the capacity level most appropriate for resource protection.
2. *Social carrying capacity*—the effect of visitors on the capacity of the resource to yield a satisfying experience to other users.

Carrying capacity varies with the type of activity involved. It is obvious, for example, that large cruising sailboats and waterskiers require more water surface for a safe and enjoyable experience than do fishermen or canoeists. This means the lake manager must have a reasonably good estimation of the activity mix on a lake in order to determine carrying capacity.

The manager must also realize that each lake has an effective boating area. In every body of water there are areas that are not or cannot be utilized for recreation purposes. Shallow water, docks and piers extending into the water, protruding rocks and/or stumps, coves, and low bridges all tend to discourage boaters from venturing into those areas. These ineffective boating areas must be deducted from the gross acreage of a lake prior to calculating carrying capacity.

It is recommended that the following basic standards be used when calculating a lake's carrying capacity:

| Type of Boat | Area Needed per Boat |
|---|---|
| Unlimited Power | 9 Acres |
| Power with Skiers | 12 Acres |
| Limited Power | 4.3 Acres |
| Nonpower | 1.3 Acres |
| Sailing | 4.3 Acres |

The standards listed above should not be applied directly to determine carrying capacity; rather, a number of factors influencing carrying capacity should be considered. It is believed that the following factors are important in influencing carrying capacity.

1. *Location of the lake in relation to population served.* Users from urban population centers are more accustomed to higher use densities than participants from rural areas. Also, users at a recreation area located near or within an urban/metropolitan area expect to see more people and tend to be more tolerant of being closer to other participants. The opposite is true for people who travel to remote recreation areas.
2. *Multiple use of water area.* Multiple use (a mix of different activities) of a lake generally causes the capacity level of each activity to be lower.
3. *Shoreline configuration.* A highly irregular shoreline generally results in a lower carrying capacity.
4. *Amount of open water.* Large, open areas are necessary to safely accommodate sailboats, unlimited power boats, and waterskiing. Thus, open areas increase capacity.
5. *Amount of facility development.* Areas with a high degree of development (restrooms, launching ramps, marinas, etc.) can carry a higher capacity than a less developed area.

When these factors, and perhaps other factors which may have an effect on a particular lake, are considered, Table 3.1 can be used to determine the appropriate standard. The table is used by adding or subtracting the appropriate factors for a particular lake.

TABLE 3.1   *Acres of Water per Boat*

| | Low | −4 | −3 | −2 | −1 | Base | +1 | +2 | +3 | +4 | High |
|---|---|---|---|---|---|---|---|---|---|---|---|
| Unlimited Power | 18 | 17 | 15 | 13 | 11 | 9 | 8 | 7 | 6 | 5 | 3 |
| Power w/Skiers | 20 | 18 | 17 | 15 | 14 | 12 | 11 | 10 | 9 | 8 | 7 |
| Limited Power & Sail | 10 | 9 | 8 | 6 | 5 | 4.3 | 4 | 3.3 | 3 | 2.3 | 2 |
| Nonpower | 2.5 | 2.3 | 2 | 1.8 | 1.5 | 1.3 | 1.1 | 1 | .8 | .7 | .5 |

Note: The methodology for determining adjusted optimum carrying capacity is based on procedures presented in *Guidelines for Understanding Optimum Recreation Carrying Capacity,* January 1977, prepared by the Bureau of Outdoor Recreation.

Figure 3.1 illustrates the system for determining carrying capacity on a lake. The formula for determining optimum capacity is as follows:

$$\frac{\text{Effective}}{\text{Acreage}} \div \frac{\text{Acre/Boat}}{\text{Factor}} = \frac{\text{Number of}}{\text{Boats}} \times \frac{\text{Relative Proportion}}{\text{of Boating Activity}} = \frac{\text{Carrying}}{\text{Capacity}}$$

FIGURE 3.1 *Determining carrying capacities on a lake.*

RECREATION AREA: ___Lake Hickory___
LAKE AREA: ___3463 Acres___          SHORELINE: ___105 Miles___
EFFECTIVE BOATING AREA: ___2190 Acres (omits 100 ft. shoreline strip)___

ACTIVITY MIX: ___Primary uses are motorboating, fishing, and water skiing___

| ACTIVITY | PERCENT OF BOATING ACTIVITY |
|---|---|
| Unlimited Power | 30% |
| Power with Skiers | 25% |
| Limited Power | 25% |
| Nonpower | 10% |
| Sailing | 10% |

FACTORS INFLUENCING CARRYING CAPACITY:

| Primary Factors Influencing Carrying Capacity | Observed Conditions | Effects of Observed Condition on Optimum Carrying Capacity |
|---|---|---|
| 1. Location (urban/remote) | Semi-rural | 0 |
| 2. Multiple Use | Three primary uses | − |
| 3. Shoreline Configuration | Irregular, relatively narrow | − |
| 4. Extent of Water Area | No major open areas | − |
| 5. Proximity to Convenience Facilities | Commercially owned facilities abundant | + |
| | Net Effect | −2 |

SUGGESTED OPTIMUM CAPACITY LEVEL FOR BOATING ACTIVITIES (See Table 3.1 for Capacities):

| Activity | Base Capacity | Adjusted Capacity |
|---|---|---|
| Unlimited Power | 9 acres/boat | 13 acres/boat |
| Power with Skiers | 12 acres/boat | 15 acres/boat |
| Limited Power | 4.3 acres/boat | 6 acres/boat |
| Nonpower | 1.3 acres/boat | 1.8 acres/boat |
| Sailing | 4.3 acres/boat | 6 acres/boat |

RECOMMENDED CARRYING CAPACITY FOR SUMMER WEEKEND DAY (Figures have been rounded off):

| Boat Type | Acreage | | Acre/Boat Factor | | No. Boats | | % Boating Activity | | Carrying Capacity |
|---|---|---|---|---|---|---|---|---|---|
| Unlimited Power | 2190 | ÷ | 13 | = | 168 | × | 30 | = | 50 |
| Power with Skiers | 2190 | ÷ | 15 | = | 146 | × | 25 | = | 37 |
| Limited Power | 2190 | ÷ | 6 | = | 365 | × | 25 | = | 91 |
| Non Power | 2190 | ÷ | 1.8 | = | 1217 | × | 10 | = | 122 |
| Sailing | 2190 | ÷ | 6 | = | 365 | × | 10 | = | 37 |
| | | | | | | | TOTAL | | 337 |

SUMMARY: The optimum carrying capacity of Lake Hickory is 337 boats.

When carrying capacities are determined in Figure 3.1, note that the numbers are rounded off.

### Additional Safety Regulations

Emphasis should be placed on all laws and regulations established by the state or local government pertaining to boating and water safety. Full cooperation should be given to appropriate law enforcement agencies as they seek to enforce these safety regulations. In addition, the managing agency should consider the following safety regulations:

1. Prohibit possession of firearms or fireworks on lake (hunters excepted).
2. Require a boat operator's license for persons operating motorboats. This regulation could best be implemented on a statewide basis. It should be noted that the National Boating Federation is very much opposed to such a regulation. That organization believes the cost and effort needed to institute such a program is too great for an unknown safety benefit. We agree that a licensing program should be undertaken only after an extensive study of the cost benefit of such a program.
3. Enforce safe load restrictions using standards adopted by the U.S. Coast Guard.
4. Regulate boat and motor size using U.S. Coast Guard and boating industry association standards.
5. Restrict swimming to designated swimming areas.
6. When hunting is allowed on a lake, restrict hunting, fishing, and other recreation activities to designated areas during hunting season.
7. On lakes that have controlled access points, require all boats to check in and out at these points.
8. Prohibit large boats (20–25 feet or more) from using small lakes (under 500–1000 acres).
9. Regulate traffic flow on heavily used lakes by having all boats travel in a counter-clockwise direction.
10. Designate no-wake speed in all appropriate danger areas around the lake (e.g., boat launching and swimming areas).

PHOTO 3.2 *This well designed buoy clearly communicates a regulatory message.*

11. Waterfowl hunters should be restricted to no more than four people in a blind, and blinds should be spaced a minimum of 500 feet apart.

## SAFETY MANAGEMENT

The managing agency should have more than a minimum regard for lake safety. Establishing safety regulations is not enough. The agency should make an effort to anticipate dangerous conditions and irresponsible acts by the public. Even under the best possible management conditions, accidents will happen and emergency situations will arise. The agency must anticipate these situations and be prepared to handle them in the best possible manner.

The majority of impoundments in the eastern United States are constructed on at least partially forested sites. When these trees are cut prior to filling the lake, the remaining stumps present a hazard for high-speed lake activity. Ideally, all underwater obstacles should be removed except for fishing areas where remaining stumps and brush will enhance fishing opportunities. On lakes where a relatively stable water level is anticipated, removing underwater obstacles to a depth of fifteen to twenty feet is an acceptable management practice. At a very minimum all obstacles should be removed around developed recreation sites and sites designated for future development. When underwater obstacles cannot be removed, they should be clearly marked. Because of the danger of fire, fueling docks or piers should be separated from boat storage facilities when marinas are built.

The managing agency should mark the lake with navigation guides using the Uniform State Waterway Marking System. Lake maps should be provided for the public, and a system for warning users of impending bad weather should be developed. A siren or warning flags are often used for this purpose.

The agency should be well prepared to handle emergency situations. When the agency employs enforcement personnel at the lake, they should assume primary responsibility for accidents and lake rescues. Personnel should be well trained in lifesaving and water safety. Rescue and medical emergency equipment should be readily available. When the lake is not manned by a professional staff, the agency should encourage voluntary and/or paid rescue squads by pro-

PHOTO 3.3  *A well equipped patrol boat is essential for enforcement of safety regulations.*

viding land at the lake for rescue stations and financial aid for the construction and operation of these facilities. Telephone and radio communications should be provided at all major access points. Land and water patrol vehicles should have radio contact with a central unit and/or the local sheriff's office.

Finally, lifeguards should be provided for all public swimming areas. Swimming areas should be clearly defined with buoy lines or marking buoys.

## ENFORCEMENT OF REGULATIONS AND ZONING POLICIES

Lacking enforcement, lake regulations and zoning policies are worthless. Lake regulations and zoning policies must be legally established, and the public must be aware of their existance. These regulations and policies must be impartially enforced, and penalties for violations must be consistently applied.

Informing lake users of existing regulations is not an easy task, particularly at lakes where people may drive some distance to use the lake. Some of the following techniques for informing the public should be useful:

- Through publications, perhaps even a special letter, sent to registered boat owners.
- Publications distributed at the lake and through an agency office (e.g., mailing along with the monthly electric bill).
- Regulations listed on back of daily and seasonal permits.
- Through the local news media.
- Signs at lake access points.

Lake regulations should be enforced by a coordinated and cooperative effort of federal, state, and local (including personnel hired by the operating agency) enforcement personnel. The lake and lake shoreline should be patrolled on a regular basis both by vehicle and by boat. Consideration should be given to supplementing this patrol by using air patrols coordinated with surface patrols and by utilizing the services of local Coast Guard Auxiliary and/or U.S. Power Squadron units. Penalties for violation of regulations should be legally established and listed as part of the regulations distributed to the public. Within any jurisdiction, regulations, enforcement, and penalties should be as uniform as possible.

## FEES AND CHARGES

More and more lake operations are depending on fees and charges for at least a portion of their operating budget. Practices adopted in relation to fees and charges will depend largely on the agency's basic operating philosophy. The amount of the charge is generally determined by the amount of service rendered by the agency (or its representative in the case of a concession operation).

Government agencies (federal, state, or local) should receive their basic operating financial support through appropriations. The agency should supplement its budget through a system of fees and charges. It is not unreasonable for any lake managing agency to operate on a self-sustaining or profit-making basis. In order for this to occur, recreation facilities must be fully developed and the lake must receive heavy recreation use. It is not practical for all lakes to be self-sustaining or profit-making. A government agency in establishing fees and charges should consider the relationship to comparable private developments and attempt to keep charges generally in line with these operations, neither higher nor lower.

Charges should be made for leases to use any agency property when made to private or commercial individuals or groups. No charges should be imposed for leases to governmental agencies or other eleemosynary organizations.

Fees and charges can reasonably be made for the following services: boat rentals, fishing, marina services (boat storage, boat launching, repairs, fuel sales, etc.), camping, swimming, merchandise sales, food and beverage sales, and group picnicking. A fee should not be imposed for family picnicking. If minimal facilities are provided (e.g., boat launching ramp only), the agency should not charge for the use of the facility. It is reasonable to require all boats on a lake to have a permit and to charge for that permit on a daily and/or seasonal basis. When a charge is made for a boating permit, consideration should be given to establishing the charge based upon the size of the boat and horsepower of the engine.

## Use of Concessionaires

A basic decision that an agency must make is whether to operate recreation facilities themselves or to extend this privilege to concessionaires through lease agreements. This decision should be based on the method of operation that will provide the best service for the public. When concessionaires are used, the agency must retain adequate control measures to ensure fair treatment for all persons wishing to use lake facilities.

Concessionaires can reasonably be expected to provide the following kinds of services: boat rentals, cottage rentals, boat repairs, merchandise sales, fuel sales, boat storage, food and beverage sales, and family camping.

Selection of concessionaires should be by competitive bidding. The concessionaire should submit a complete operating plan, and selection should be based on expected quality of service to be rendered as well as financial considerations. The agency should protect concessionaires by not allowing too many to operate on a lake. The agency's lease agreement with the concessionaire should include, but not be limited to, the following considerations:

- If the concessionaire is expected to develop facilities (buildings, docks, or piers, for example) as a part of the agreement, a long-term lease (up to twenty years) with a cancellation clause if the concessionaire (or agency) does not live up to the lease agreement should be granted.
- The agreement should be based on a percentage of gross with a guaranteed annual minimum payment to the agency.
- It should require an annual audit of the concessionaire's books by the agency.
- The agency should annually review and approve prices to be charged by the concessionaire.
- Sanitary standards expected of the concessionaire should be established, and standards should be enforced by frequent inspections by an agency representative.

*Concession contracts and cooperative agreements with public and private organizations.* It is appropriate for the lake managing agency to enter into concession contracts with private firms and into cooperative agreements with governmental and nonprofit agencies to provide recreation services at their lakes. Primary emphasis in these agreements and contracts should be to provide water-based recreation facilities and programs as a part of the agreed-upon recreation plan for the lake. When the demand for water-based recreation has been met in a particular region, it is appropriate for the lake managing agency to enter into agreements to provide other types of recreation activities such as ball fields and golf courses.

Agreements with public agencies should give preference to established park and recreation agencies with demonstrated capability to develop and manage a resource-based recreation area. Other contracting agencies should demonstrate their ability and intent to have or secure manpower, equipment, and other resources necessary to maintain and operate the proposed recreation area. The contracting agency or organization should be responsible for the development of a site master plan. The lake managing agency should assist the contracting agency in site development by providing basic site services such as launching ramps, public parking, internal roads, and utilities.

A contract prospectus for the development of recreation facilities and services should be required prior to any agreement between agencies. The contract prospectus can be initiated by either the lake managing agency, a public agency, or a private organization. The contract prospectus is a document that includes, but is not limited to, at least four sections of information as shown in the following example.

### SAMPLE CONTRACT PROSPECTUS

Section I. Introduction
  1. Purpose of the bid or offer.
  2. General characteristics of the initiating agency or organization.
  3. Identification and description of the specific lake and, if possible, the specific site where the proposed development would take place.
Section II. Facilities and Services
  1. Facility description and service needed.
  2. Reason for the service.
  3. Rates to the public—fees and charges.
  4. Contract limitations.
  5. Personnel rights and privileges.
  6. Supervision and inspection by the lake managing agency.
  7. Park or facility rules and regulations governing the facility.
  8. Site master plan, development plans, building plans, etc., applicable to the proposed development.
Section III. The Bid or Offer
  1. Selection of the applicant by the lake managing agency.
  2. Length of contract.
  3. License fee—gives the proposing agency or bidder the right to occupy certain space. The fee is often high enough to cover the costs of capital improvements, if any.
  4. Franchise fee—percentage of gross receipts by the bidder for the privilege of doing business on the lake managing agency's property. (Applicable only to private organizations or businesses.)
  5. Data to accompany bid or offer to include financial condition (balance sheet), experience, personal references, proposed timetable, and cash flow position. (Applicable only to private organizations or businesses.)
  6. Submission of bids or offers to include how, when, where, and security deposit requirements.
  7. Qualification of applying agency or organization as well as qualifications of individuals responsible for the proposed facility.
  8. Condensed net worth statement—balance sheet.
Section IV. Contract Draft Form (Terms and Conditions)
  1. Contract recital.
  2. Description and location.
  3. Term (length) of contract.
  4. Time of operation (season and hours).
  5. Payments (if any) and means of monitoring accounts.
  6. Provision of utilities.
  7. Buildings and equipment.
  8. Maintenance of property.
  9. Sanitation.
  10. Merchandise for sale.
  11. Personnel.
  12. Permits.
  13. No lease to second party.
  14. Assignability.
  15. Advertising.
  16. Alterations to property.
  17. Inspections.
  18. Damage to property.
  19. Insurance.
  20. Violations of contract and surrender.

# PERSONNEL

Practically all functions of lake management require qualified personnel to execute them. Personnel then become a key to implementation of the agency's goals and objectives. The indispensable functions of planning, coordinating, evaluating, protecting, educating, and enforcing must be accomplished directly or indirectly by personnel who are qualified, properly trained, and motivated to carry out their responsibilities in a professional manner.

Whenever possible, a recreation division should be established within the operating agency. The management of recreation facilities and programs should be vested in this division. The agency should employ persons with park and recreation administration degrees and/or experience to manage or assist with management of recreation activities on lakes. In-service training programs should be established or provided for agency personnel involved with recreation activities. These programs should include training in first aid, water safety, public relations, and law enforcement.

# PUBLIC RELATIONS AND EDUCATION PROGRAMS

The agency must make every effort to maintain good public relations with the recreation user. A good public relations program means that the agency must communicate with the public and make every effort to keep the user informed of conditions and activities at the lake. Efforts should be geared to make the user's recreation experience as pleasant as possible. Education programs will add to the user's enjoyment by adding to his skill and knowledge.

The agency can keep the public informed through the local news media, agency publications, and personal contact by agency staff (e.g., talks and color slide presentations to civic and youth groups). Daily information should include changes in lake elevation, fishing conditions, special recreation opportunities, and educational programs. When hiring new recreation staff persons, particularly enforcement personnel, consideration should be given as to how well they will relate to the public. The agency should provide in-service training programs for all employees who come in contact with the public in the performance of their jobs.

The agency should carry out a variety of educational programs and encourage other organizations to conduct educational programs at the lake. A good method of implementing educational programs is to assign the responsibility to one staff member for program development and to work with outside volunteer groups. In order to emphasize the importance of the litter problem, the agency should consider providing special educational efforts on this topic. The agency should also consider the periodic distribution of litter bags to the public.

# DEVELOPMENT OF AREAS AND FACILITIES

A major influencing factor on the recreation user's experience is the variety, quantity, and quality of facilities provided by the agency. Facilities must be carefully planned and functionally designed to meet users' needs. Facilities should be considered a means by which more satisfying recreational opportunities can be enjoyed by a majority of participants. In providing water-oriented facilities, the agency must also plan appurtenant facilities such as access roads, adequate circulation roads, and parking.

Considerations related to development of recreation areas and facilities should include the following:

- Recreation areas and facilities should be developed only after a cooperative planning effort has been accomplished. The agency should utilize the best available planning resources. These resources may include the agency's professional planning staff (when existing), professional park and recreation planners, architects, professional recreation staff, and other technical personnel.

- Public access and circulation roads should be developed through careful coordination with the highway department. Unattractive private development on access roads should be controlled by a local or regional lake zoning ordinance.
- Directional signs for specific developed recreation sites should be provided by the Highway Department. Well-maintained signs should be provided by the agency on property under its jurisdiction.
- Parking facilities to accommodate normal weekend use should be provided by the agency. An overflow area should be provided to handle peak load use. Parking attendants should be used on heavy-use days to ensure optimum use of parking areas.
- When interest is sufficient, special use areas should be developed. For example, if interest in sailing is sufficient, the agency could develop a launching area to be used exclusively by sailing craft. Competitive waterskiers also have special needs. An area of a lake could be marked off for their use, or times could be established for them to use a section of the lake.
- Swimming areas should be developed to provide the following facilities: beach with clearly defined swimming area, bathhouse, restrooms, and hot showers.
- Both picnic sites and campsites should be developed back from the shoreline, but still within visual contact of the lake, keeping the shoreline available for all to use.
- Where practical, consideration should be given to the development of camping and/or picnic areas that are accessible only by boat.
- Boat launching ramps should be provided with a 12 percent slope, forty-foot parking spaces nearby, a wide turning area near the ramp, and loading docks for the convenience of boat passengers.
- Providing piers for fishing at selected areas around the lake may help prevent shoreline erosion.

## MAINTENANCE OF RECREATION AREAS AND FACILITIES

Well-designed, esthetically pleasing, and well-constructed access roads, parking areas, and recreation facilities can be ruined by poor maintenance. A facility of lesser quality may be enhanced by good maintenance while an excellent facility that is poorly maintained may be rejected by users. Lake patrons have every right to find a clean, neatly kept area for their outings. Sloppy maintenance is a sure sign of poor management.

General maintenance standards must be established for the maintenance of areas and facilities. These standards should be incorporated in a well-conceived maintenance plan which serves as the blueprint for the entire maintenance program. Since the developed recreation sites are often widely scattered and long distances from each other in terms of road mileage and driving time, self-contained maintenance and utilization of contractual maintenance agreements are both appropriate.

Dumping solid waste on agency property is a problem with which a majority of lake managers are confronted. This is a particular problem in some rural areas that are not served by either governmental or private solid waste collection agencies. In areas where dumping solid waste on agency property is a serious problem, it should be controlled by cooperative efforts of the agency and local law enforcement personnel.

General trash and litter deposited by recreation users is also a serious problem because of the large acreage and many miles of shoreline associated with the normal large lake. Litter and trash on shore at other than designated recreation areas should be controlled by:

- Giving litter bags to all boaters when they register to use the lake.
- Allowing participants to picnic and fish from the bank only at designated areas.

- Barricading all roads and access points not designated as recreation areas.
- Distributing trash receptacles at strategic points.
- Conducting litter pick-up campaigns and contests.
- Sponsoring educational programs with an antilitter theme.

## SUMMARY

Large lakes provide marvelous recreation opportunities for millions of Americans. The lake manager's challenge is to manage these lakes in such a way that the recreation experience will be enhanced rather that ruined. This chapter has considered some of the major issues that confront the lake manager. Solutions to management problems are complex and difficult to deal with. However, attention to the principles and practices addressed in this chapter should lead to improved water-oriented recreation opportunities for large lake users.

# 4

# MARINAS

The popularity of recreational boating is well documented in Chapter 1. In 1984, nearly 13.5 million recreational boats were enjoyed by 67.2 million U.S. citizens. Of those boats, 74 percent were of a type that required facilities or services provided by marinas.

Retail expenditures on boating is currently over $12.3 billion per year, which explains why the private sector provides nearly 400,000 boat slips and over 12,000 launching ramps to the boating community. In addition, thousands of ramps are provided by public agencies such as the Corps of Engineers, Tennessee Valley Authority (TVA), state fish and game agencies, and local governments.

The development of reservoirs by the Corps of Engineers, Bureau of Reclamation, TVA, and private power companies has resulted in over 99 percent of the U.S. population living within fifty miles of a publicly owned freshwater lake, and about 33 percent within five miles of a lake. Most of the lake and reservoir shoreline is publicly owned, making most of the 12 million acres of water surface accessible for boating. One result from the construction of each reservoir is the surfacing of a latent demand for water-based recreation. New boat dealerships open to provide would-be mariners with a variety of equipment to enjoy on the new impoundment, while marinas develop on the lakes' shoreline to facilitate the continuous needs of the boaters.

## SCOPE OF SERVICES

The word *marina* can result in a wide range of mental images, depending on the person's experiences. To one boater a marina might mean a remote launching ramp and bait shop, while to another it is row after row of piers with ocean-going yachts, numerous support buildings, a beach or pool, and strange-looking cranelike structures to launch or retrieve boats.

Either of these concepts can be accurate. The size, shape, and scope of services of each marina should be uniquely suited to the needs of local boaters. The origin of the word *marina* is credited to the National Association of Engine and Boat Manufacturers (NAEBM), an organization that in 1979 joined with several other trade organizations to form the National Marine Manufacturer's Association. In 1928 the NAEBM first used the Latin word *marina* to describe a modern boat basin which provided facilities for berthing, supplying, and servicing all types of recreational watercraft. A marina may provide any of a variety of services for boats and boaters including the following: wet (in-water) and dry (out-of-water) berthing; launching; automobile parking; dockside electricity and fresh water; telephones; restrooms and showers; laundry, repair, and maintenance facilities; retail sales areas for marine supplies, food, ice, and fuel; facilities for pumping waste from boat holding tanks; a marine supply shop with boat hauling, repair, and storage service. Ancillary facilities might include such amenities as swimming pools; restaurants; shopping areas for groceries, drugs, and clothing; and access to airplane, rail, or bus terminals.

All of the above services need not be supplied by the marina itself. Adjacent businesses might provide some of the services. In planning a new marina, however, the availability of these and other basic services should be determined.

The majority of marinas are privately owned and operated as profit-making enterprises. Marinas on lakes developed by the Corps of Engineers, TVA, or private power companies are usually concession agreements between the agency and a private entrepreneur. In those cases the owning agency provides the land and access roads while the concessionaire develops the marina at his expense. The development of support facilities and services (e.g., parking, utilities, launching ramps, etc.) may be negotiated, depending on the circumstances. It may be unreasonable, for example, to expect a private developer to construct several miles of road to a site selected by the owning agency for the marina.

## Ownership of Marinas

Many marinas are owned and operated by state and local park and recreation agencies. The Kentucky and Tennessee state park systems operate marinas in those parks developed on Corps of Engineers or TVA lakes. Communities of varying sizes can be found to own and operate marinas. Some are developed on inland lakes or rivers while others are located in coastal areas. The cities of Miami, Fort Lauderdale, and St. Petersburg in Florida; San Diego and Long Beach in California; and Seattle, Washington, have developed and operate some of the largest marinas in the United States.

Any marina, whether developed and operated as a private business or as a public service by a municipality, should follow proven management concepts for a successful operation. Five factors originally recommended by the National Association of Engine and Boat Manufacturers are as follows:[1]

1. *Facilities must be adequate.* The types and appearance of marina facilities should be adequate for the future as well as the present. Materials should be selected that will be functional and attractive for the boaters and yet capable of withstanding the type of environmental forces that can occur in that particular location. Prefabricated dock systems designed for protected inland lakes might resemble matchsticks following a coastal storm.

2. *Provision must exist for expansion.* The provision for future expansion is not a luxury but a necessary hedge against changing times and technology. The marina's expansion potential depends upon the land surrounding the marina, the availability of adequate waterfront area for additional rental docks, present and future access roads, water rights, and financing.

3. *Accounting and management procedures must be adequate.* Some marinas are known to show net profits of 25 to 30 percent while others continually lose money. The motivation and resources of the operator may play a major part in determining the marinas' profit picture, but efficient accounting and management procedures are critical to achieve maximum potential profit.

4. *Facilities and services must be compatible with patrons' needs and desires.* Marinas take on a unique personality that reflects the interests and priorities of its patrons. Some marinas cater to fishermen and waterskiers while others attract ocean-going cruisers. Some marinas provide full-service maintenance yards while others concentrate on simply renting berths. There is no magic formula as to a package of services that will guarantee success. Rather, an understanding of the types of basic facilities and services needed by local boaters, plus amenities and prices that will attract them to the marina will go a long way toward having a successful marina operation.

5. *There must be a good relationship between the marina and the community in which it is located.* The success of a marina may be based on its relationship with the community in which it is located. Proposed marina developments must comply with established plans and zoning regulations if they are to receive the support of civic leaders and officials. In most cases a marina is a welcome addition to a community with an undeveloped waterfront. It may be possible to combine other proposed developments (e.g., parks, outdoor theatres, civic centers, motels, golf courses, etc.) with the marina. Another action that could prove to be mutually successful might be to lease an area of the marina to a yacht club whose present accommodations may be inadequate or nonexistent. This will help a group of local boaters in solving their problem while providing the marina with guaranteed income during the initial years of operation.

A final point favoring marina development is that, done well, it can result in dramatic increases in local revenue. Land values around the marina will most likely increase, other marine support businesses may develop, and cruising boaters may be enticed to visit the community and take advantage of local restaurants and shops.

**PHOTO 4.1** *The Harbor Town Marina at Hilton Head, S.C. provides the focal point for luxurious homes and shops.*

## PLANNING CONSIDERATIONS

The development of a marina requires a significant financial investment. Millions of dollars may be spent in constructing basic facilities before the first dollar is collected. For that reason alone, the developer should avoid rash investments and careless assumptions that may lead to a needless waste of capital and unnecessary frustrations.

### Feasibility Study

The ultimate success of a marina complex depends on an analysis of numerous environmental, social, and financial considerations. The analysis of those considerations may be in the form of a feasibility study. Such a study should be developed by a professional planning consultant.

While the process is not beyond the capabilities of the proposed developer, a carefully selected recreation planner or marina consultant possesses both objectivity and experience that are important ingredients for a sound feasibility study.

In completing the feasibility study, it is imperative to remember that the primary objective is to determine the *need* for a marina, not to justify a predetermined decision to develop the marina.

The content of a marina feasibility study might include the following:

1. Inventory of existing marina facilities.
2. Type of marina.
3. Determination of need.
4. Potential sites.
5. Methods of financing.
6. Revenue potential.

*Inventory of existing marina facilities.*   This should include both private and public marinas, yacht and boating clubs, public launching ramps, maintenance and repair businesses, and boating supply services. The geographic area for the inventory of existing facilities will vary, depending on the proximity of the proposed marina to areas of large population. In large metropolitan areas the supply of marina facilities can seldom keep pace with demand. In those situations the key is to examine the type of boating activity that is prevalent (e.g., power boating, cruising, sailing, fishing, etc.) and to determine whether existing marinas are full with a waiting list for berths, or whether there is an abundance of slips, moorings, repair and maintenance yards, and other marine facilities and services.

In more remote areas the importance of determining the competition for a proposed marina becomes a matter of critical concern. Day use boaters will normally travel up to fifty miles with little regard for the time or cost of travel. Owners of large, cruising-type boats are willing to travel considerably farther because once there, their boat provides their accommodations as well as their leisure pursuit. In both cases, however, the assumption is made that there are no other boating areas of equal quality closer to major population areas than where the proposed marina would be located.

*Type of marina.*   The type of boating activity in a given area is determined, in part, by existing environmental conditions. The type of water body, water access needs, and water depth may eliminate certain boating activities while facilitating others. Table 4.1 provides general environmental requirements for various boating activities.

*Determination of need.*   This is one of the critical periods in the life of a marina. Upon it will hinge all decisions from the types of boats it will service to the size, location, and methods of financing the development. The proof of need is the strongest selling point in acquiring necessary financial resources for the development of the marina.

While the services available at a marina can vary considerably, it is important to know that it is the basic services that generate the greatest amount of revenue. With few exceptions the rental of berths produces a larger amount of revenue than other services that might be provided. Exceptions would be a marina that has a large boat sales business or a facility that has few moorings but a large service and maintenance operation. In coastal communities the supply of berths can seldom keep up with demand. Through a quick check with existing marinas, one can get a good indication of the need for additional dock space. If numerous berths are currently available, and if the fee structure is in line with other marinas, perhaps another type of development should be considered. On the other hand, if all but a few berths are full, and the marinas have long lists of boaters waiting for a slip, the need for additional moorings is obvious.

TABLE 4.1 *General Requirements of Marinas by Boat Type and Boating Activity.*

| Boat Type and Activity | **Water Body Type** – Canal | River | Bay | Coast | **Water Access Needs** – Open ocean or bay within 5 miles | Suitable fishing waters within 5 miles | Inlets, islands, beaches for safe anchorage within 20 miles | Inlets, islands, beaches for safe anchorage within 10 miles | Access to suitable open water within ½ mile | Pond or channel at least 1 mile wide | Pond or channel at least 5 miles wide | **Minimum Channel Depth** – 4 feet | 6 feet | 8 feet | **Special Attributes Needed** – Relatively protected waters | Few shoreline hazards |
|---|---|---|---|---|---|---|---|---|---|---|---|---|---|---|---|---|
| Commercial fishing and deep sea charter dock | | ● | ● | ● | ● | | | | | | | | | ● | | |
| Long-distance powerboat cruising | | ● | ● | ● | ● | | ● | | | | | | | ● | | |
| Long-distance sailing | | ● | ● | ● | ● | | | ● | | | | | | ● | | |
| Estuarine fishing | ● | ● | ● | | | ● | | | | | | | ● | | | |
| Local powerboat cruising | | ● | ● | ● | ● | | ● | | | | | | | ● | ● | ● |
| Day sailing Ⓢ and racing Ⓡ | ● | ● | ● | ● | | | | ● | ● | Ⓢ | Ⓡ | | ● | | | ● |
| Water-skiing and water sports | ● | ● | ● | | | | | | ● | ● | | | ● | | ● | ● |

*(Coastal Assessment Guidance Handbook,* U.S. Environmental Protection Agency, Washington, D.C., 1984)

If a marina development is being considered for a new reservoir, there are no other facilities to examine and the need for marine services is difficult to determine. In cases where there is an extensive population base within a fifty-mile radius, and little competition from other water resources, the concept of "latent demand" usually applies. That is, while people may not express their desire for marine service facilities, and even where boating does not currently seem to be popular, the development of a reservoir will lead to an increase in boat sales and activity. In short, the development of the reservoir creates a demand for boating and other water-based recreation.

The needs analysis should analyze the market area population to determine if they have characteristics indicating they are likely to participate in boating activities. Research shows that boat ownership and use increases with income and education. Comparing local demographic data to state and national statistics will provide another indication of need.

*Potential sites.*   A number of factors must be explored in selecting potential sites for the marina complex. This selection will hinge upon boat population area; land value and cost; zoning restrictions, waterway requirements; availability of public utility services; accessibility and compatibility with surrounding environment and land use; clearance with appropriate federal, state, and local government agencies; and competition from existing marinas. In the investigation of possible marina sites, the availability of municipal, state, or federal lands should be considered. Land may be available on a lease or rental basis to provide recreational facilities for the public. This is common practice on Corps of Engineers reservoirs owned by the federal government and under control of the Corps. In addition, the proposed site must be protected from severe currents and prevailing wind and wave action; and the water must be of a depth to accomodate the types of boats anticipated. While it is a common practice to dredge navigable channels and boat basins, it is an expensive undertaking that should be minimized as much as possible.

**PHOTO 4.2**   *Matheson Hammock Marina is well protected and is readily accessible by land or water.*

Photograph provided by Miami-Metro Department of Publicity and Tourism, Miami, Florida.

*Methods of financing.*   Privately owned, commercially operated marinas are developed at the expense of the owner or owners. Some are privately owned by individuals; others are in partnerships or syndicates. Many marinas are family businesses, which allows the benefit of minimizing overhead costs; however, financial resources for expansion or improvement are usually limited.

Public marinas are financed in a number of ways. As with most large expensive capital improvement projects, however, marinas are most commonly developed through the sale of general obligation or revenue bonds. General obligation bonds have an advantage over revenue bonds in that there is not the pressure to pay off the debt through marina receipts. On the other hand, policy-making boards are often more inclined to approve a project that will pay for itself (revenue bond) than to pass on the burden to citizens through a tax increase.

While not as significant as in the past, there are still matching grants available for land acquisition and recreation capital improvement projects. The Land and Water Conservation Fund, in particular, has enabled a number of communities to develop excellent marina facilities. State recreation planning offices are usually knowledgeable as to the status of this and other funding sources.

*Revenue potential.* The majority of marinas are privately owned and commercially operated to make a profit. While the primary mission of the public marina is service, rather than profit, the fees charged should be in line with similar services at commercially operated marinas and the marina operation should not be subsidized with public tax monies.

No two marinas are exactly alike in the mix of services provided. As a result, it is difficult to generalize as to which phases of the operation will produce the greatest revenue. In addition, there may be a big difference between the amount of revenue produced through a service or facility and the actual net profit realized. Commercially operated marinas, for example, may generate well over 50 percent of their total revenue from the sale of boats and engines but may have a profit ratio of only 10 percent. Slip rentals, on the other hand, may generate considerably less gross revenue than the sale of boats and engines but have a much greater profit ratio. Table 4.2 shows the results of a financial study of 190 marinas located in all sections of the country. While the study is somewhat dated, there is reason to believe that the profit ratio and gross income figures may still be applicable to a contemporary marina.

TABLE 4.2   *Average Marina Income Sources*

| Facility | % Profit Ratio | % Gross Income |
|---|---|---|
| Slip Rentals | 39.2 | 19.4 |
| Winter Storage | 27.4 | 10.0 |
| Repairs/Overhauling | 26.7 | 11.7 |
| Sales: | | |
| New Boats/Engines | 16.4 | 10.5 |
| Used Boats/Engines | 8.8 | 8.2 |
| Marine Supplies | 22.8 | 13.1 |
| Petroleum Products | 15.1 | 10.1 |
| Boat Rentals | 15.2 | 10.1 |
| Restaurant and Bar | | 4.4 |
| Groceries/Ice/Vending | 14.9 | 2.1 |
| Bait & Tackle | | 3.7 |
| Boatel Units | | 2.6 |
| | | 100.0 |

(*Marina Costs/Revenues Study—1974,* National Association of Engine and Boat Manufacturers, New York.)

An analysis of the figures in the marina financial study might provide direction in determining the types of facilities and services to offer at a proposed marina. Marina planners, however, should be careful to avoid oversimplification of potential revenue sources. Careful consideration should be given to labor, materials, merchandise, and maintenance costs that accompany each area of operation. Table 4.3 shows the direct operating costs chargeable against various areas of operation for all selected marinas and the resulting gross profit obtained from each.

It is interesting to note that the top three gross profit revenue operations all involve boat mooring and storage. An agency or investor that wants to develop a marina that will maximize

TABLE 4.3  *Cost-to-Revenue Analysis*

| Revenue Source | % Labor | % Materials, Merchandise, Maintenance | % Gross Profit |
|---|---|---|---|
| Slip & Mooring Rental | 11.3 | 17.4 | 71.3 |
| Winter Storage | 25.2 | 12.6 | 62.2 |
| Dry Land Storage | 20.0 | 30.0 | 50.0 |
| Food | 23.9 | 41.4 | 34.7 |
| Service & Repairs | 43.3 | 32.9 | 23.8 |
| Sale of Hardware, Paint, & Parts | 13.4 | 69.6 | 17.0 |
| Sale of New Boats & Engines | 3.6 | 82.0 | 14.4 |
| Sale of Used Boats & Engines | 7.5 | 79.2 | 13.3 |
| Boat Rentals | 4.3 | 84.5 | 11.2 |
| Fuel & Lubricant Sales | 11.0 | 78.4 | 10.6 |
| Other (Ice, Bait, Fishing Tackle, etc.) | 18.1 | 43.4 | 38.5 |

(*Marina Costs/Revenues Study—1974,* National Association of Engine and Boat Manufacturers, New York.)

revenue while minimizing the number of employees and other costs of operation might concentrate on providing slips, dry-land storage, dry-stack storage, and other moorings. As the developer expands the scope of services and facilities, development costs and overhead will increase, in some cases dramatically. The percentage of profit may not be as significant for a sales or repair operation as for berth rental, but the actual income might be too high to ignore. If there is a good market for boat sales, the marina has the potential of generating considerable revenue. Likewise, the provision of a quality repair and service yard can produce considerable revenue. However, it is important to keep in mind that maintaining an inventory of new boats, constructing show-room and maintenance buildings, and the purchase of travel lifts to launch and retrieve boats are all expensive propositions. In addition, there is the added expense of hiring repair and service personnel to support each operation.

*Cost of development.*   Since there are so many different aspects involved in marina development, it is necessary to separate the various phases into a more readily understandable and controllable plan. This separation should follow the natural order of development stages which follow: (1) dredging and filling, (2) bulkheads and breakwaters, (3) piers, floats, catwalks, pilings, and related facilities, (4) buildings and equipment, (5) utilities, roads, parking lots, and landscaping, (6) engineering, planning, inspection, and supervision costs, and finally (7) a reasonable estimate of materials, labor, operation overhead, and contractor's profit. It is also wise to allow a percentage for cost increases, unexpected contingencies, and forgotten or desired additional services and facilities.

Actual development cost figures can only be determined by persons familiar with the local area since a variance in cost will occur in two sites side by side due to terrain, tides, winds, and numerous other factors. A marine engineer should be involved in marinas where water fluctuation, wave and wind action, tidal activity, or swift currents are present. His fee will be repaid many times by the savings effected through his knowledge and efforts.

*Method of operation.*   The majority of privately owned marinas are operated by the owners themselves. Many are relatively small family businesses where outside help is hired only when there are not enough family members to do all of the work, or where a special skill is needed, such as a mechanic or fiberglass specialist.

In some cases the owner has no interest or time to be directly involved in the day-to-day operations due to other commitments, distance from his residence to the marina, or lack of experience. In those situations, a manager might be employed to oversee the marina operations.

A number of resort developments that include marinas among their amenities utilize the services of a marina management firm. The advantage of this approach is that the management firm can provide marina services without being burdened with maintenance and routine operational details involving the facilities, or the purchasing of products for resale.

Municipalities in the process of planning marina developments are faced with the option of self-operation or leasing. Governmental managing authorities are often faced with this problem, and strong opinions exist on either side of the question. Many municipal marinas are managed successfully by the local park and recreation department while others are leased to private entrepreneurs. In the final analysis the primary concern should be which system will be most equitable and beneficial to the public.

The process of conducting a feasibility study is essential for any group considering the development or expansion of a marina. In addition to determining the need for a marina, which is critical if the marina has any chance to succeed, it also helps to identify the best location, method of financing, scope of services, size, types of features to be incorporated, and revenue projection.

## PLANNING, DESIGN, AND DEVELOPMENT

### The Master Plan

Once the decision has been made to proceed with the marina construction, a master plan should be prepared to guide the development. The master plan should be prepared by a marina consultant, architect, or engineer. The firm should be experienced in planning marinas and should have staff who are knowledgeable in the areas of engineering, recreation management, and planning. The master plan should incorporate what was learned from the feasibility study relative to type of boater who will be served. The plan should show all items of proposed construction and improvement in onshore and offshore areas, such as roads, buildings, equipment, slips, and extent and location of dredging and disposal areas. The master plan serves as a guideline for preparing design and construction drawings, and for making quantity and cost estimates. The master plan will prove to be a necessary document in connection with permits, authorizations, financing, public meetings, and promotional activities.[2]

The master plan should include a timetable for the development of various marina facilities. It is generally advisable to develop the marina in stages over a several-year period so that completed facilities can be opened to provide operating experience and income for the owner. An obvious consideration is to develop basic facilities first (e.g., rental slips, restrooms, roads, and parking) that will accommodate boaters while generating significant financial returns.

Many phases of marina development and operation are similar to other types of construction and business. However, there are a number of unique considerations within the experience of a majority of investors. As a result, the National Marine Manufacturers Association has compiled a checklist of common pitfalls in marina planning which may be avoided by their recognition and incorporation. They include the following:

1. Careless land title searching, especially in old established areas, may overlook limitations of use placed on specific tracts.
2. Underestimating private local interests may lead to opposition. An example might be opposition from members of a yacht club or residential area with waterfront facilities on the same body of water. They may not look with favor on the influx of new traffic.
3. Locating the marina on a site that has a land-to-water ratio of less than 1¼ to 1 will hinder future expansion and make it difficult to provide all the facilities needed to attract and hold the modern boater.
4. Spending too much capital on purchase of land, regardless of its suitability for marina construction, will unduly delay profitable returns on the total marina investment.

5. Shelving practical planning for esthetic considerations can lead to the provision or location of facilities not convenient to patrons.

6. Planning of future facilities in detail long before they are scheduled to be built is a waste of time and money. Changing concepts of marina development indicate that it is best to develop detailed facility plans just prior to construction.

7. Minimizing the value of an engineering consultant, or considering these services expendable while planning, will result in a second-rate master plan or costly delay in performance of the key investigatory work.

8. Using inferior construction materials will lead to future economic problems that will have to be faced while the marina is in operation. Not only will the replacement of low-grade construction prove costly, but there will be a loss of income while the defective facility is being replaced. The axiom, "if you don't have time to do it right the first time how do you expect to find time to do it over again" applies to this guideline.[3]

The authors suggest that one of the NMMA checklist items should be altered and two additional items added: Item five suggests that esthetics or beauty be sacrificed for functional considerations. While functional layout is vital for efficient management and convenience, the modern boater is growing in sophistication and IS concerned with the appearance of the marina where considerable leisure time and money is spent. Where the natural beauty of a site has to be compromised, or where the original site is lacking in attractiveness, the developer should provide esthetically pleasing buildings, structures and landscaping to add to the quality of the boating experience. Two items that should be added to the above list are: (1) Check with the Corps of Engineers, as well as with state and local officials to determine permits that must be secured prior to proceeding with the development. Some states take months to process applications. In cases that involve destruction of an aquatic ecosystem, it may not be possible to get a permit. (2) Be sure that an experienced recreation planner is involved in the master plan process. A recreation planner can maximize the efficiency of the marina complex, oftentimes resulting in considerable financial savings, add to the quality of the recreation experience of the boaters, and avoid costly maintenance problems for the manager.

A number of organizations can be of assistance in providing information and materials that may be of value to marina developers:

- *Coast and Geodetic Survey:* This agency has available planimetric maps, coast and harbor charts, and current and tide tables.
- *Coast Guard:* The local Coast Guard district office can be helpful in fact finding during the planning phase. The Coast Guard publishes a number of books and pamphlets on navigation and safety that may prove helpful.
- *Geological Survey:* The U.S. Geological Survey (USGS) has topographical maps that include much of the land surrounding our waterways.
- *Lake Survey.* The Lake Survey of the Corps of Engineers prepares and sells navigational charts of the Great Lakes, the St. Lawrence River, Lake Champlain, and the canal system of New York state.
- *International Oceanographic Foundation:* This agency conducts studies of marine life and is an excellent source of information regarding forms of marine life that can do damage to marine pilings and structures.
- *National Fire Protection Association:* This agency provides information on fire protection for boatyards and marinas.

### Guidelines for Development

The range of services provided by marinas is nearly endless (see Table 4.4). The privately owned, commercially operated marina is concerned about maximizing revenue production while meeting the boating and personal needs of its clientele. Some public marinas have the same goals as their private counterparts, while others may sacrifice profit in the name of service. We will concentrate on those basic services and facilities that are normally required at a typical marina. They include:

- Boat launching and hoisting facilities.
- Boat mooring and storage facilities.
- Ancillary facilities (fueling dock, parking, repair and maintenance facilities, etc.).

**TABLE 4.4** *Marina Services and Facilities*

| Marina Services | |
| --- | --- |
| **Water Related** | **Land Related** |
| Boat launching | Boat sales |
| Mooring service | Boat repairs |
| Water taxi service | Marina supply sales |
| Transient boat service | General supply sales |
| Waste collection | Trailer storage |
| Fueling | Parking |
| Boat towing | Overnight accomodations |
| Fire and rescue services | Food service |
| Navigation and weather information | Concessions |
| | Utility service |
| | Recreational services |
| **Marina Facilities** | |
| **Water Related** | **Land Related** |
| Open and covered mooring | Boat building and repair |
| Boat launch ramp | Dry boat storage |
| Marine railway | Trailer storage |
| Crane lift | Restaurant |
| Drydock | Motel |
| Fueling pier | Picnic areas |
| Anchorage areas | Convenience store |
| Marine service station | Boat washing |
| Entrance and exit channels | Parking |
| Swimming area | Swimming pool |
| Water skiing course | Camping |
| Basin flushing system | Beach area |
| Storm and wave protection | Club room |
| | Marine supply sales |
| | Public toilets and showers |
| | Recreational facilities |

(*Coastal Marinas Assessment Handbook*, U.S. Environmental Protection Agency, Washington, D.C. 1984.)

Before going into detail about the various facilities mentioned above, it may be of value to the reader to review some of the terms that are part of the working vocabulary of boating and marina activity:

- *Bulkhead*—a structure or partition built to prevent erosion of the land behind it.
- *Dock*—Strictly defined, a dock is the water area in which a boat lies when "made fast" (tied up) to a shore structure. In boating, however, the term *dock* is usually applied to structures bordering the water area in which the boats lie.

- *Dry-stack storage*—a system of steel racks, several layers high and usually enclosed in a building, in which boats are stored.
- *Mooring*—A semipermanent anchorage installation, consisting of a heavy anchor, chain, and a mooring buoy.
- *Pier*—A structure that projects outward from the shoreline.
- *Pilings*—long, heavy timber or a section of concrete or metal driven into the harbor bottom to which craft may be made fast or which support a structure.
- *Slip*—A berthing space between two piers.
- *Wet storage*—an in-water storage area for boats.
- *Wharf*—A structure parallel to the shore.

***Boat launching and hoisting facilities.*** Marinas usually provide some launching and hoisting equipment but leave the heavy handling work to the repair and storage yards. The type of facilities or equipment installed depends upon two factors: (1) the type of boat the marina will service and (2) the proximity of boat yards capable of launching and retrieving boats of the type and size that the boating area will accommodate. Some of the more common facilities are as follows:

*Launching ramps.* A marina should provide ramps for launching boats from trailers. While some areas are fortunate to have a hard sand surface of a suitable slope to launch a boat from a trailer, the marina developer should anticipate having to construct a concrete ramp. It is usually a good policy to avoid locating launching ramps in the same area with rental berths. The ramp should, however, be located where it can be seen from the marina manager or dock master's office. Locating the ramp near the fuel dock often works well since both require close supervision and neither is totally compatible with rental berths.

Rigging and derigging areas should be provided near the launching ramp, usually in the form of an extra lane, to prevent boaters from tying up the launching ramps for long time periods. The launching ramp should be constructed at a 12 to 15 percent slope. Less than 12 percent may result in insufficient depths to float the boat off the trailer, while a slope that is too steep may make it difficult for cars to have adequate traction to pull the boat up the ramp from a dead stop. The width of the launching lane should not be less than twelve feet with a curb constructed on each side to prevent miscalculating drivers from backing off the sides of the ramp. The approach area to the ramp should provide sufficient space so that the inexperienced driver will have plenty of room to maneuver his trailered boat.

Day use launching facilities should have multiple lanes and adequate parking to accommodate the anticipated use. It normally takes five to six minutes to launch or retrieve a power boat; ten to fifteen minutes for a sailboat. Forty to sixty parking spaces are required for each launching lane. Each space should be ten feet wide by forty feet long to accommodate both the vehicle and the trailer. Parking spaces at a 45-degree angle are easier to use than right angle parking. Pull-through parking spaces are easiest to use but expensive in space utilization and construction costs. Overflow parking can be provided on relatively flat grassed areas. Day use launching areas should provide sanitary facilities within 300 feet of the ramp at approximately one fixture per sex per 150 cars.[4]

All launching ramps should have courtesy docks to aid boaters in controlling their boat while another member of their boating party is parking or maneuvering the car and trailer. A sand or grass beach adjacent to the launching ramp will prove to be a convenience for boaters to pull up their craft during the day and for launching car-top boats.

If significant sailboat use is anticipated, special attention should be given to the placement of ramps and courtesy docks relative to prevailing wind direction. If possible, avoid locations where the prevailing wind pushes the boat onto the ramp. Ramp sites with prevailing winds blowing from the land to the water, or parallel to the shoreline, are preferred.

*Hoisting facilities.* Many marinas find a need for facilities and equipment to launch and haul out boats where a ramp is not acceptable. This is particularly true for marinas that cater to large boats that cannot be car-trailered, but it is also true for marinas where ramps are not feasible or where boats are stored on racks (stack storage).

**PHOTO 4.3** *A courtesy dock assists boaters in launching and retrieving boats.*

Large boat repair or storage yards may have a variety of mechanical devices for moving, launching, and hauling boats. Boat-handling equipment might range from marine railways, cranes, and derricks to fork lift trucks and sling lift hoists. Not every marina is in need of heavy-duty boat handling equipment. If adequate repair or storage yards are available nearby, and if adequate water or land area is available, a marina may decide to concentrate on the provision of wet slips or storage of boats on trailers. On the other hand, marinas that provide boat sales, repair, and maintenance will find hoisting facilities to be a necessity.

Mechanical hoists of any type are expensive pieces of equipment. Marinas that find an extensive need for hoists can realize a high net profit from that operation. Conversely, a poorly located and slow operating hoist will guarantee a constant net loss.

Sling-type hoists are well suited for handling boats weighing up to sixty tons and more. Of course, the larger the hoist, the greater the cost, so care must be taken to select a model that will handle the boats in that area. To buy a larger hoist would be a waste of money.

A relatively recent approach to small boat storage is *stack storage*. This involves multilevel racks where powerboats are stored, launched, and retrieved by a stacker crane or fork lift truck. The type and size of the crane or fork lift is determined by the weight and length of the boats being stored. More detailed information on stack storage systems is provided later in this chapter.

*Boat mooring and storage facilities.*   To most people a mental image of a marina consists of row after row of beautiful yachts floating effortlessly among neatly spaced pilings or docks. In fact, for most marinas, the rental of wet berths or slips constitutes the heart of marina profit. One of the primary reasons that rental berths can be so profitable is that, once constructed, only a minimal amount of maintenance should be required for a number of years. On the other hand, if poor decisions are made regarding materials, construction, or anchoring systems, the results can be devastating. One bad storm, a severe freeze, a flood, or a drought can totally destroy a marina's best source of net profit, not to mention the boats being moored at the pier or docks.

The storage of boats takes many forms. Larger vessels generally are left in the water year-round, particularly in areas where hard freezes seldom occur. Smaller vessels are usually hauled out and stored in buildings or in an open, protected area preferably fenced and lighted. Some of the more common mooring and storage facilities are as follows:

**PHOTO 4.4** *The mobile slingtype hoist is a popular and efficient means of launching and retrieving large watercraft.*

Photograph courtesy of Marine Travelift, Sturgeon Bay, Wisconsin.

- Wet slips (open and covered)
- Moorings
- Dry storage (storage yards and stack storage)

*Wet slips.* The more convenient facility for storing a boat is the wet slip. The vessel is already in the water; therefore, a minimum amount of effort and time is needed to get underway. Wet slips require piers and pilings or docks to provide easy access for the boater and a secure mooring for the vessel. Marinas catering to larger boats will normally provide water hookups, night lighting, and electrical hookups for each slip. Some may even have sewage hookups, but this service is normally restricted to major metropolitan marinas that allow owners to live aboard their vessels.

Coastal marinas normally provide piers or walkways to accommodate the boater in gaining access to his boat and pilings to secure the craft in its slip. Piers may be constructed of wood pilings driven into the harbor bottom, or jetted into the bottom with high pressure water hoses, with flooring added to create a dock. The pilings must be pressure treated with creosote, salt, or other chemicals to prevent decay and to provide protection from wood borers. Concrete piers are common in some areas and make durable structures for combating the severe coastal environment.

Pilings are commonly used in areas where the water is of limited depth and where water level fluctuation is usually restricted to a few vertical feet. Enough piling should protrude from the water surface to facilitate boat security during occasional flooding. Wood pilings resemble utility poles that have been driven as far into the bottom as necessary to provide a stable and secure mooring.

Well-protected coastal marinas have the option of using floating dock systems in place of piers. Numerous prefabricated floating dock systems are commercially available. The advantages of floating dock systems make them a good choice for inland marinas in that they can be used in waters of any depth and will rise and fall with water fluctuation.

**PHOTO 4.5**   *Electrical and water hookups should be provided where large boats are moored.*

Meeco Docks, MacAlester, Oklahoma.

The problems confronting the inland marina developer are different, but no less challenging, than those facing his coastal counterpart. The challenge of designing and constructing wet slips and docks in harsh saltwater and tidal areas may be replaced by lakes and rivers beset with severe water level fluctuation, deep water, and fast-moving currents.

The creation of lakes and reservoirs by federal agencies has resulted in the development of numerous marinas, involving a variety of arrangements between government agencies and private entrepreneurs. However, the primary reasons for creating the impoundments often makes marina design and construction a significant challenge. The major justifications for reservoir development are flood control, electric power production, and water supply. All three create conflicts with recreation use due to the variation of water level to store flood waters from the drainage basin or to maintain water flowage downstream. Floating dock systems are utilized in reservoirs that experience significant water level fluctuations.

Floating docks are constructed of a variety of materials. Many earlier docks utilized steel drums for flotation; however, they have a limited life span and have been outlawed in some states. Modern dock flotation systems are constructed of a variety of materials ranging from styrofoam blocks and fiberglass tubs to steel and hollow concrete pontoons. More important than the type of flotation unit, however, is the dock superstructure and anchoring system.

A dock with wet slips may project several hundred feet from the shoreline. It may be a singular unit, but most likely it will consist of modular components that are attached to one another with specially manufactured hinges. As many boats as possible will be berthed at each dock, some of which may weigh many tons. One can imagine the stress placed on a dock system when hit by a severe storm. The force of the wind on the dock structure and the boats is enormous. Add pounding wave action, and it is easy to see why the superstructure and anchoring system is so critical for the dock system to last year after year with minimal maintenance.

Prefabricated dock systems normally have a superstructure of steel or wood. It is wise to specify hot-dipped galvanized steel or pressure-treated wood to guarantee years of low-maintenance use. Laminated wood is considerably stronger than standard board and timber construction. All bolts and metal hardware should be of high-strength galvanized or stainless steel. Wood flooring should be attached with bolts or screws rather than nails.

**PHOTO 4.6** *Prefabricated floating dock system during installation. Utility line trough is covered upon completion. Slip collar allows vertical movement but prohibits lateral movement.*

Anchoring systems vary with the hydrographic conditions of the site. A widely used system utilizes steel pipes (spuds) or wood pilings to hold the floating docks in place. Slip collars mounted to the dock allow vertical variation but prohibit lateral movement. Some of the limitations of such systems are deep water and rock bottoms. If such conditions exist, the developer may decide to use large anchors and winch systems or to tie the dock to the shore with cables. The anchor and winch system is relatively simple but requires adjustment with water level fluctuation. If the dock is tied to shore with cables, care must be taken to attach the cables low enough on the dock superstructure to avoid contact with boat hulls, keels, and propellers. In reality, a combination of any or all of the three anchoring techniques may be utilized at various parts of one dock system.

The construction of docks is no place to skimp on quality or to challenge the forces of nature. Marinas should be located in a naturally protective setting or within a man-made breakwater. Major dock manufacturers have structural engineers that can specify materials and anchoring systems for specific applications. Since those engineers are employed by the dock supplier, it is a good policy to secure a second opinion from an independent structural engineer.

Many marinas provide covered slips to add protection from the damaging effects of sun and weather. Covered slips are particularly popular for powerboats but impractical for sailboats.

*Winter storage.* In warm climates, wet storage of boats during winter months does not present much of a problem. In areas where freezing temperatures are a deterrent to wet storage, steps must be taken to protect the vessel as well as the dock system.

Floating dock systems, particularly those in open areas, may have to be removed from the water during winter months. In some cases, it may be possible to disconnect floating docks from the headwall and tow them to nearby well-protected areas until the fear of a hard freeze has passed.

PHOTO 4.7   *In colder climates, docks may have to be stored out of the water during winter months.*

PHOTO 4.8   *The result of ice movement on a dock system not removed for winter.*

An alternative to removing docks and boats from the water during winter months is a deicing system. The concept behind de-icing systems is to circulate warmer water from the bottom of the slip to the top, thus keeping ice from forming. There are two basic de-icing systems that are commercially available: (1) A compressor carries air through tubing at low pressure to the bottom of the slip. Rising bubbles carry warmer water from the bottom to the top. (2) A fanlike device either floats in the area to be kept free of ice or is mounted to a piling or dock structure. The unit circulates warm water from the bottom to keep the water surface from freezing.

*Moorings.* If wet slips are limited in number, but protected water surface is abundant, the marina developer may install mooring buoys. Mooring buoys are anchored individually or in a series connected to a heavy cable on or near the bottom of the harbor. Mooring buoys are preferred over docks by some sailors because the boat is able to adjust to changing wind direction and always meets waves and wind with the bow of the vessel. Two obvious limitations to mooring buoys are (1) electric and water hookups are usually impossible, and (2) another boat must be utilized to get to and from the moored craft.

Owners of small sailboats, canoes, and fishing boats may prefer to leave their crafts secured at a beach. A pipe mooring rail can be provided far enough up the beach to allow boat owners to secure their crafts out of the water. If shoreline areas are abundant, the beach mooring is an inexpensive and convenient method for accommodating small watercraft.

*Dry storage.* In the case of smaller vessels, storing the craft out of the water may be preferred by boaters. A well-secured storage yard allows a boater to leave his craft on its trailer, rigged and ready to be launched as needed. Storage yards are popular among sailers who can leave the mast up, thus eliminating a time-consuming task for boaters who lack an adequate storage area at their residence for boats and trailers, and for others who are not comfortable towing a boat over the highway.

A popular dry storage concept for small powerboats is the *stack storage* system. Stack storage involves racking boats three to five levels high in cradles mounted on a steel superstructure. Most stack storage facilities are within large warehouse-type buildings. Launching and retrieval are achieved by means of a specially designed crane or a fork lift truck that maneuvers the boat out of its bay and either places it directly in the water or transfers the vessel onto a marine elevator which is lowered into the water. The system is capable of handling boats from sixteen feet to approximately twenty-six feet in length.

Dry-stack storage is a concept that has a number of advantages over other boat storage systems. Stack storage is a high-density system that requires a minimal amount of expensive waterfront area. One marina operator posts the advantages of stack storage as its only advertising effort. Because those advantages are generic to the concept of dry-stack boat storage, it might be well to mention them: "No refinishing, no sun fading, no collection growing on the bottom of your boat, no expensive cover to buy, no messy ropes, no dew, frost, or blowing rain, no bugs, birds, or dust; your boat locked in every night so you can leave life preservers, skis, ropes, and personal belongings aboard without worry." It's an impressive list guaranteed to attract the attention of any boater.

While dry-stack boat storage has considerable potential for marinas developed to serve smaller powerboats, careful study should be made to be sure it will be cost effective. The cost of developing a stack storage system requires that most storage cradles will be full and that a large enough fee can be charged to pay capital and operating expenses and generate a profit. This is usually the case in a high-population boating area but may be a problem in rural areas where alternative storage systems are available at lower fees.

*Ancillary facilities.*    The modern marina may include a wide array of services and facilities to meet the needs of the boating customer. The combination of facilities at any particular marina should be carefully determined to satisfy the unique needs in that area. It is wise to begin with basic facilities and consider more specialized amenities as interest and need develops. The most basic needs, boat launching and storage, have already been discussed. Other basic

PHOTO 4.9 *Interior of a typical small boat stack storage building.*

PHOTO 4.10 *A forklift truck launches, retrieves, and stacks a small boat.*

support facilities may be necessary, depending upon the type of boats serviced and the services provided by competing marinas.

Basic support facilities might include a fueling dock, clubhouse with restrooms and showers, repair yard, boat and/or marine supply sales area, parking, and waste pump-out facility. Other support facilities that can be found at selected marinas include a marine railway, crane lift, dry-dock area, anchorage area, swimming pool, waterskiing course, trailer storage, restaurant, motel, laundry, picnic area, playground, boat washing area, campground, and other recreation facilities.

Planning and development guidelines for support facilities normally found outside the marina complex are available elsewhere. However, several suggestions are provided relative to those support facilities unique to marinas:

- *Fueling dock.* The fueling dock should be conveniently located near launching areas and wet slips. Locating fueling areas at the outer end of rental docks or adjacent to a restaurant or snack bar should be avoided due to the danger of fire and explosion, as well as the problem of fouling the water with fuel and oil spills. The fueling area should have adequate maneuvering room for boats. Pressurized water and fire-fighting equipment should be present. If the marina services larger power and sailboats, it will be necessary to provide diesel fuel as well as gasoline.
- *Parking.* Seldom will more than 50 percent of the boaters be present at the marina at any given time. Many boating parties will have more than one car at the marina. Therefore, parking capacity is determined by $1\frac{1}{2}$ cars $\times$ $\frac{2}{5}$ the marina capacity, or .6 cars per berth.[8] Additional parking may be needed to store boat trailers.
- *Pump-out station.* If at all possible the sanitary pump-out station should not be located at a high-use area. Rather, it should be located at the fringe of the marina complex, possibly adjacent to the repair yard. In many cases the pump-out station will be found at one end of the fueling dock. While not ideal, this does provide a convenient multi-purpose service area. A water hose should be available to assure cleanliness.

**PHOTO 4.11**   *A sanitary pump out station may be necessary where larger cruising boats are abundant.*

Photo courtesy of United Flotation Systems, United McGill Corporation, Columbus, Ohio.

- *Repair yard.* Boat repair yards are often unsightly and can be dangerous for those unfamiliar with their operation. The repair yard must have access to the waterfront as well as to service buildings. It should be out of view of the average marina user. Boat-handling equipment should be selected to meet the needs of marina users.
- *Service building.* A number of services can be provided in a centrally located marina service building. The complex might house offices, sales areas, restrooms, showers, laundry, lounge, and food service. The service building should be located near the access road to the marina yet within view of the fuel dock and waterfront.

PHOTO 4.12  *Boat repair yards should be out of view.*

## OPERATING CONSIDERATIONS

Marinas are leisure service businesses that depend on satisfied consumers for their success. Successful marina operators have learned that their business is unique and that the key to success is in their ability to recognize that quality service provided by courteous personnel can be costly, but far less expensive than the void left by a disgruntled boat owner. It is important for the marina operator to be constantly aware that he is serving people who seek recreation and sport. The marina operator can help the boater in gaining maximum pleasure out of one of the most valued commodities in his world: leisure time with his boat.

The provision of a well-rounded program of marina services and facilities requires the consideration of a great number of details. From the viewpoint of the marina operator, four major points of concern are as follows: (1) the functional organization and staffing of the marina and its facilities, (2) methods to employ in setting service charges and fees, (3) leasing marina facilities and service operations to private businessmen, and (4) operational and safety regulations over boating activities in the marina.[5]

### Functional Organization and Staff

Basic management responsibility for marina operations should be vested in the chief administrative officer or his authorized representative. In terms of major management responsibilities, the chief administrative officer (1) formulates budget proposals that parallel the governing body's decision regarding the type and level of services to be provided at the marina; (2) establishes and maintains a system of reports and controls to evaluate marina operations and services; (3) procures necessary staff and makes contractual arrangements for services; and (4) generates necessary operational and financial data to develop recommendations to the governing body which will help to protect the investment of the owners, limit their financial liabilities, and assure their capability to continue providing public recreational boating services.

The selection of the right staff to operate the various facilities and provide services at the marina is probably as important to the success of the marina as having the optimum number and type of services and facilities. An efficient and courteous staff is a valuable resource which will contribute greatly toward successful marina operations. The marina operation may encompass a wide range of services. While the chief administrative officer is responsible for overall operations, he must delegate authority and responsibility to permit the marina to carry on under somewhat functional lines. The number and type of employees involved in marina operations will vary depending on the number, type, and level of services provided, and the extent to which marina facilities and services are leased to private entrepreneurs. Excluding those operations, which are usually leased, such as the boat and motor sales shop and restaurant, most marina operations fall into three functional areas which are handled by (1) a harbormaster (or dockmaster), (2) a yard manager, and (3) a repair shop manager.

As suggested by its title, the position of harbormaster is concerned with activities offshore of the bulkhead. Among the chief responsibilities of this position are:

1. Allocating berth and slip assignments.
2. Supervising fuel and oil sales.
3. Enforcing safety regulations.
4. Handling the rental of boats, dock lockers, and other dockside facilities.
5. Providing information on services available to patrons and making arrangements with other departments or agencies to provide such services.

The yard manager is the onshore counterpart of the harbormaster. The major responsibilities of this position include:

1. Assigning dry boat-storage areas.
2. Arranging for the pickup and delivery of patrons' craft.
3. Enforcing parking and safety regulations on the marina premises.
4. Providing information on services to patrons and making necessary arrangements with other departments and agencies to perform those services.

The repair shop manager is responsible for servicing and repairing boats and engines of patrons as well as servicing craft for resale, if boat brokerage is a function of that marina. In cases where refinishing, refitting, and boat rebuilding make up an important segment of the marina's activity and income production, it may be necessary to create a department for these purposes which is separate from the repair shop.

While the separation of the three functional responsibilities facilitates an ideal marina organizational structure, it should be borne in mind that two or more of the functions might be assigned to one capable individual, particularly in a smaller operation, or in cases where difficulties are encountered in recruiting capable persons to fill all three positions.

## Setting Service Fees and Charges

Slip rentals, storage fees, proceeds from repair services, and sales of boats and motors provide nearly 85 percent of the average marina's gross income. Uniform slip rental rates and storage fees, which account for nearly one-third of the average marina's gross income, cannot be suggested for two basic reasons. First, initial development costs, levels of service, and operating costs will vary from one marina to the next. Since these costs are the chief bases used to determine service fees and charges, variances in these costs make it impossible to guarantee uniform slip rental fees and charges. Second, in the case of municipal marinas, it is difficult to determine the extent to which they are self-supporting or subsidized by tax revenues. Generally, fees and charges at municipally operated marinas should be in line with those at private marinas that are open to the general public. To charge less gives the private operator justification for accusing the public marina of taking away his business.

To establish service fees and charges in a systematic fashion, it is necessary to review operating and development amortization costs and distribute those costs on a use basis by purpose of expenditure or major function. To do this, general accounting records must be constructed and maintained to certain minimum standards to assure the availability of accurate cost information and facilitate analyses with a minimum of duplicate effort. First, all expenditures should be recorded on the basis of an established object classification that follows acceptable accounting standards. The four basic elements of operating costs include:

1. *Direct labor,* charged to the unit or job to which it provided the service.
2. *Equipment expenses* which are usually reflected in an hourly "equipment rental" charge.
3. *Materials and supplies* which can be directly charged to the jobs as they are purchased and used.
4. *Overhead expenses* which may include the cost of administration, supervision, insurance, employee benefits, amortization of development costs, utilities, and other such expenses which cannot be conveniently charged directly to specific jobs or operations.

Second, timekeeping and payroll procedures which are used in the general accounting system must be maintained in sufficient detail to make cost allocations possible. Third, the general accounting system should provide an adequate system for controlling and issuing materials and supplies to make it possible to allocate these costs to specific jobs or operations.

*Determining cost centers.* In a typical marina, cost centers to which expenses must be allocated might include (1) slips and docks, (2) dry boat-storage areas, (3) repair shop, (4) retail departments, and where present, (5) food and beverage.

*Distributing personnel and equipment costs.* Personnel assigned to marina operations will most likely be involved in a variety of activities. This will require the distribution of personnel costs among two or more cost centers. One way of accommodating this is the use of a daily time card. Payroll cost analyses for direct labor charges can then be made for distribution to the various cost centers.

As in the case of personnel, a system must be developed to allocate equipment usage at each cost center. As mentioned above, expenses for equipment usage should be based on a derived "hourly equipment rental rate" to facilitate the allocation of equipment acquisition, maintenance, and depreciation expenses to cost centers.

*Distributing Costs of Materials and Supplies.* Materials and supplies, purchased directly or taken out of stock, should be allocated to the various cost centers as they are used. This requires a requisitioning procedure to assure the correct allocation of material costs to the proper cost center. As the need arises for materials or supplies, a requisition from stock or a purchase requisition should be processed which indicates the purpose, activity, or facility to which these costs are to be allocated.

*Distributing Overhead Expenses.* The cost of administration, employee benefits, supervision, insurance, and amortization of development costs are principal overhead costs which must be allocated to cost centers for purposes of fixing service fees and charges. Costs of employees' benefits and supervision can be apportioned in a reasonable manner on the basis of the percentage of direct labor costs allocated to each of the cost centers. Amortization of development costs may be allocated on the basis of the percentage of capital invested in slips and docks, storage areas, repair shop, and other cost centers. Once sufficient experience has been gained in the allocation of costs to various services, rates should be set at the beginning of each year based on the prior year's results. Monthly reviews of costs and revenues derived from marina services should be made to make certain that overhead is being kept in line and services are not being priced out of the reach of patrons.

### Leasing Marina Facilities and Services

In the operation of a marina, a number of different services and facilities may be offered to the public. In some situations, because of a shortage of development funds, it may not be possible to provide all of the services or facilities which the boating public may need or desire. In other cases, a facility or service may have produced financial losses year after year. There is also the possibility that the operating organization lacks the necessary knowledge and personnel to provide a particular service. Each of the above situations poses a dilemma for the marina owner and for the chief administrative officer. Failure to provide a particular facility or service which the boating public feels it needs may endanger the financial base of the entire marina operation. The financial base of the marina may also be endangered to a degree by the failure of service fees or charges to support a facility or service; however, the financial base may be endangered to a far greater degree by the loss of patron good will if maintaining patron good will depends on retaining the "loss-producing" service or facility. In such circumstances, it may be advisable for officials to consider the possibility of leasing a part or all of the marina facilities through a concession agreement with a private business operator or developer.

While certain advantages may accrue to a municipally operated marina by leasing facilities, officials should also be aware of some of the disadvantages. First, by leasing all or part of its marina operations, the municipality's control over marina operations is lessened somewhat. Second, there are no guarantees that the municipality will not be vulnerable to poor concession operators. This is a particular danger to guard against in any long-term lease arrangement. Normally, the lessee will want a long-term lease to amortize any sizeable investment in facilities or equipment. A long-term lessee who is the subject of complaints may end up doing more harm to a municipal marina's reputation than any good which the municipality might get from a concession agreement with the lessee. In view of these possibilities, some suggested guidelines are presented below to assist marina officials in developing lease or concession agreements which will help to minimize the disadvantages to the municipality.[6]

1. *Selection of firm or individual.* After deciding which facilities and services are needed, officials may seek out private firms or individuals who may be interested in submitting a bid to furnish the facility or service required by detailed specifications. In considering this approach, officials should be reasonably sure that it is economically feasible for an individual or firm to provide the facility or service required by the specifications, and that there is a sufficient number of capable and interested firms or individuals to assure the municipality receiving bids that are truly competitive.

Another approach is to formulate a description of the facilities or services needed at the marina and request interested parties to submit their best proposals to meet these needs. This system provides the bidders with a greater degree of latitude to draw on their expertise and knowledge of the concession business. If this approach is used, officials should require proposals to reflect the type of facility or service which is proposed; the price structure for services; types and quality of merchandise to be sold; the extent of capital investment needed and the manner in which the investment is to be provided; the length of the contract deemed reasonable to recoup capital investment; the percentage of gross income that would accrue to the municipality; and the final disposition of property or installations upon termination of the lease or concession.

Regardless of which approach is used, officials should require bidders to submit information which will be helpful in assessing their capabilities in carrying out the terms of the lease or concession agreement. Included among these factors are performance records of similar business ventures, credit references, operating statements, statement of assets and liabilities, and references to overall experience in that line of business. The inclusion of these factors in the specifications will make it possible to consider the best bid or proposal on a number of other important factors besides general factors such as "most money to the municipality or owner."

2. *Term of agreement.* It is generally advisable to select a term of years that is long enough to make it worthwhile for a private firm or individual to devote resources and energies to the project. In a situation that involves a considerable amount of outlay or capital investment, the bidder may require, and the municipality or owner should be prepared to consider the approval of a fifteen to thirty-year lease. A one to five-year term lease may be considered for the operation of a facility or providing services if the lessee does not make any sizeable investment in facilities or major equipment.

3. *Construction of facilities.* The lease or concession agreement should be specific about the obligations of the parties for the construction of facilities. For the protection of the owner, agreements should require the approval of all plans and specifications for any construction on the marina site. Secondly, all plans and specifications for construction should be required to be in accord with all state and local codes and ordinances. Third, the agreement should provide a specific and reasonable timetable for the submission of construction plans after the agreement is signed. A timetable for the beginning and completion of construction should be submitted after the approval of plans and specifications. Lastly, the agreement should describe the disposition of title to construction upon completion of construction and termination of the agreement.

4. *Financial arrangements.* The agreements should describe in detail the financial contributions of each party toward the construction of fixed improvements and the concession to be made to the municipality or private owner for the privilege of operating a facility or providing a service at the marina. Terms of the concession are generally stated in terms of flat, sliding progressive, or sliding regressive percentage of gross receipts. Also, the agreement should specify the time, manner, and condition of payment of monies to the marina.

5. *Lessee's records.* The owner should insist in all agreements that the lessee be required to keep accurate and complete records and accounts of all transactions in the operation of its business. Provision should be made for an annual independent audit to be submitted to the owner.

Two additional points are worthy of mention. The municipality or private owner should reserve the right to install on leased premises any devices or machines for accounting or auditing purposes. Secondly, the municipality should require the lessee to keep all records, books, accounts, and other data which are needed to establish the lessee's gross receipts and deductions for a reasonable time period after payment is made to the owner.

6. *Lessee's insurance coverage.* The lessee should be required, under the terms of the agreement, to carry specified amounts of liability, property damage, fire, and workers' compensation insurance.

7. *Controls over operation.* A wide variety of controls which may pertain to the lessee's operations can be included in the lease or concession agreement. Some of the more common examples include (1) the lease agreement should prohibit the lessee to sublet any part of his operation without prior approval of the owner; (2) the municipality should exercise some control over the rates charged by the lessee; (3) lease or concession agreements generally require the lessee to perform repair and maintenance work within an enclosed structure and maintain the leased premises in neat and orderly fashion; and (4) the written consent of the municipality or private owner may be required for the erection of signs, advertising, or other promotional devices for the lessee's facilities or services.

8. *Termination provisions.* In accordance with accepted principles of contract law, leases or agreements should include provisions for termination and cancellation, and options for the renewal of the lease or agreement. In recognition that unforeseen contingencies may arise, especially in long-term contracts, provision should be made for interpretation of the agreement in light of possible changes in conditions which may affect its operation.

## Safety Considerations

For boaters who are familiar with boating laws and regulations, have skill in the operation of their craft, understand the potential dangers that are inherent in boating, and utilize common sense, the marina can be a lifetime source of pleasure. However, marinas and boating, by their very nature, deserve serious attention to be sure that the enjoyment of the activity is not interrupted by an unnecessary accident or incident. In addition to the safety concerns that are present with any water-based activity, the marina is laden with equipment and trappings that, if not used properly, can be the cause of accidents, injury, and the loss of life. Boat rigging, dock lines and cleats, gasoline and diesel engines, fuel storage tanks, and strange-looking boat-handling equipment are all necessary to the marina operation. Yet, each can create havoc for careless boaters and their guests. It is the responsibility of the marina owner, developer, manager, and each user to do everything reasonably possible to minimize the occurrence of injuries and accidents.

**Boating rules and regulations.**   On navigable waters of the United States, federal laws and regulations controlling boat equipment and operations prevail. The states enjoy concurrent jurisdiction with the federal government on federal waters within their boundaries, and authorized peace agents may enforce state laws. The U.S. Coast Guard is the chief federal law enforcement agent, although the Coast Guard has no authority to enforce federal law on purely state waters. It should be noted, however, that a state law cannot conflict with the federal law on the navigable waters of the United States and still be valid. The federal laws are paramount.

In addition to federal statutes, the U.S. Coast Guard regulations and special regulations of the U.S. Army Corps of Engineers, the National Park Service, and the Bureau of Sport Fisheries and Wildlife prevail in waters under these agencies' jurisdictions. Handbooks of state and federal boating laws are available from most federal agencies and from each state.

**Fire protection and prevention.**   One of the most important areas of concern to the marina manager is fire prevention and protection. A number of organizations have recognized the peculiar fire hazards inherent in marina operations and have formulated suggested codes and regulations. Included in this list is the National Electrical Manufacturer's Association, the American Gas Association, the National Fire Protection Association, and the Building Officials Conference of America.

Boats utilizing either municipal or private marinas should be constructed and equipped to conform to standards of the U.S. Bureau of Marine Inspection of the U.S. Coast Guard, and the Fire Protection Standards for Motor Craft prepared by the National Fire Protection Association. Adherence to these regulations and applicable state and local codes will add materially to the safety of the harbor and fleet by reducing fire hazards to a minimum.

*Boating safety.*   The marina manager should formulate and promulgate sets of local rules and regulations to govern maneuvering, berthing, servicing of boats, and the conduct of boat owners and marina users. In general, rules should define the authority of the marina's management and establish standards for safety, health, and comfort of marina patrons. While no one set of rules is suitable for all localities, a number of basic provisions can be proposed for consideration by local officials. The National Marine Manufacturers Association provides a detailed listing of recommended regulations in *Marinas, Recommendations for Design, Construction and Management.*[7] An abbreviated list of suggested regulations is presented below:

*Suggested Marina Regulations*
1. The word *operator* is used to indicate any person authorized to represent the actual owner of the marina. The word *tenant* is used to indicate the owner of a boat legally within the marina or any person who is otherwise using the facilities.
2. When a boat enters the marina, it immediately comes under the jurisdiction of the operator and shall be berthed or anchored only where ordered and maneuvered as directed.

**PHOTO 4.13** *Fire protection equipment should be readily available.*

*Photo courtesy of United Flotation Systems, United McGill Corporation, Columbus, Ohio.*

3. Only pleasure boats will be admitted.
4. Houseboats will (or will not) be permitted.
5. Commercial fishing boats, boats for hire, and other types of commercial craft will (or will not) be admitted.
6. No advertising or soliciting will be permitted on any boat within the marina.
7. Boats not marked or identified as required by law will not be permitted within the marina.
8. Tenants will record their home and business addresses and local telephone numbers as a mutually protective measure.
9. All boats shall be tied up in berths or at moorings in a manner acceptable to the operator or shall be removed from the marina; or the operator, after notice to the tenant, will adequately tie up the boats and assess a service fee.
10. Boats shall be in a seaworthy condition and not constitute a fire hazard, or they shall be removed from the marina.
11. The operator shall have the right to inspect all boats in the marina to determine seaworthiness and adherence to local and federal fire and safety requirements.
12. Tenders and dinghies shall be stored on board larger vessels, on land, or in water as directed by the operator. They shall be marked or named and such identification recorded with the operator.
13. No boats within the marina shall be operated in excess of the established speed limit.
14. No swimming, diving, or fishing will be permitted within the marina (except as specified in the lease).

15. Boat owners shall not store supplies, materials, accessories, or debris upon any walkway and shall not construct thereon any lockers, chests, cabinets, steps, ramps, or other structures except with permission of the operator.

16. No refuse shall be thrown overboard. Garbage will be deposited in containers provided for that purpose, and other debris shall be placed where specified by the owner.

17. Tenants shall use discretion in operating motors, generators, televisions, radios, or bilge pumps so as not to create a nuisance.

18. Disorder, depredations, or indecorous conduct by a tenant or his visitors that might injure a person, cause damage to property, or harm the reputation of the marina shall be cause for removal from the marina of the boat in question.

19. Vessels entering the marina during an emergency shall be reported immediately by their owners to the operator.

20. No repairs (or repairs to a certain extent) may be made to boats while in slips. Such repairs shall be made only in areas specifically set aside for such work and upon approval by the operator.

21. Slip rentals; mooring charges; storage rates; and water, electric, telephone, and launch service shall be strictly in accordance with published schedules. All rentals for space shall be paid in advance. No refunds (or refunds according to a prearranged schedule) will be made. No subleasing of slips or transfer of boats between slips will be allowed except upon prior permission of the operator.

22. When an owner expects to have his boat out of his slip for more than one week (or other designated period of time), he shall so notify the operator in advance, who may lease the slip for other purposes during this period.

23. The operator is not responsible for any losses on or damages to boats in the marina. Each owner will be held responsible for damage which he may cause to other boats in the marina or for damage to any structure. Any boat which may sink in the marina shall be removed by the tenant.

24. Boats in the marina shall be equipped with lights and be operated according to the Rules of the Road and the Navigation Laws of the United States.

Any set of rules adopted should be given to each boat owner. At large marinas the rules should be prominently posted. The rules should be made a part of the agreement for leasing a slip or mooring space.

***Employee safety.***   Employees are exposed to the inherent potential dangers of the marina environment on a continual basis. The knowledgeable, experienced, and safety conscious marina worker is familiar with the unique health and safety considerations in constant evidence and treats each with respect. However, the marina manager should make every effort to orient and train new employees to conduct their activities in a safe manner.

Municipal marinas should consider sending all staff who will be handling water craft to the closest National Aquatic School conducted by the American Red Cross. These programs are conducted in a highly professional manner and can teach even experienced personnel new ideas. All Red Cross instructional programs place the highest priority on skill development under the safest possible circumstances. Marinas that provide boating instructional programs should also make sure that their instructors complete the appropriate Red Cross Instructor/ Trainer program. While it may not be difficult to find a potential instructor with years of quality experience, there is no guarantee that he can transfer that knowledge to others. Red Cross Instructor/Trainer programs make no assumptions about the knowledge and experience of their students; an important consideration when introducing newcomers to the basic skills of any form of boating.

## SUMMARY

The purpose of this chapter was to review the critical concerns in planning, constructing, and managing marinas. Marinas are necessary wherever major water resources are available for boating activity and may be provided by private entrepreneurs or government agencies. Marinas are major business enterprises that require significant capital expenditures, sound business and management practices, and an understanding of the importance of recreation and leisure time to the boat owner. Marina managers should be familiar with the costs involved in purchasing and maintaining boats of various types and sizes. Only then will it be possible to realize the importance that boating plays in the lives of marina users. Good planning, quality construction and sound management should guarantee the long term success of the marina as a business while providing an enjoyable leisure outlet for the boating public.

## NOTES

1. National Association of Engine and Boat Manufacturers, *The Modern Marina,* New York, 1963, p. 10.

2. *Ibid.,* p. 37.

3. *Ibid.,* p. 40.

4. Fogg, George E., *Park Planning Guidelines Revised,* National Recreation and Park Association, Alexandria, Va., 1981, p. 132.

5. Moran, Henry, *Marina, Finance to Function,* Revenue Sources Management School, North Carolina State University, Raleigh, N.C., 1968, p. 2.

6. *Ibid.,* p. 8.

7. Chamberlain, Clinton J. *Marinas, Recommendations for Design, Construction and Management,* Volume I, Third Edition, National Marine Manufacturers Association, Chicago, Ill. 1983, pp. 163-165.

# 5

# BEACHES

The bathing beach has become the most widely used recreational facility in this country, and probably in the world.[1] Evidence of this is the preference of coastal settings for resort and other commercial recreation developers, and the popularity of beaches for weekend outings and family vacations.

Swimming beaches are provided by private operators as well as public agencies. By 1975, nearly 3 million linear feet of improved beaches were being provided by private operators.[2]

The combination of an abundance of water resources in the United States, the popularity of swimming, and the natural attraction people have for shoreline settings makes the efficient and safe management of swimming beaches essential. The development and management of beaches varies by type, size, location, and number of visitors. Beaches may be divided into three categories: (1) coastal or ocean-front, (2) inland-lake, and (3) riverfront.

Coastal beaches and Great Lakes beaches have similar problems of construction, operation, and maintenance. Inland lakes vary dramatically in size and condition. Large natural lakes usually have a stable water level, while lakes constructed for flood control or hydroelectric purposes often experience considerable fluctuation. The construction of swimming beaches must take this and other factors into consideration.

Beaches constructed on rivers have unique maintenance and operation problems created by currents and fluctuating water levels. Few river beaches have proven to be satisfactory and, where possible, other alternatives should be sought out.

## ESSENTIAL BEACH FACILITIES

All swimming beaches have certain essential facilities that are common whether the beach is an ocean-front facility in a major city or a privately operated swimming pond in a rural area. In addition to the provision of a beach area that is a safe and pleasant environment, there is generally a need for visitor parking; a bathhouse with changing areas, restrooms, and showers; and a food and beverage concession. The following guidelines may be of value in planning a new swimming beach development or in evaluating an existing facility.

### Beach Sites

*Coastal and Great Lakes beaches.* Swimming beaches on ocean shorelines, bayfronts, and the Great Lakes should be located where a natural site for a beach exists. While some construction may be necessary in the beach area, a suitable site should have a gently sloping natural sand beach and an underwater area relatively free of rocks, marine formations, and other hazards. Wind and water action which erode shorelines and displace sand, causing wash-outs and undertows, should be taken into account when selecting a site for a swimming beach.[3] There are many examples of beach areas where efforts were made to stabilize the shoreline through the construction of groins, breakwaters, and jetties. In most cases those efforts have proved to be short-term solutions, eventually resulting in erosion of the swimming beach itself or of an adjacent beach above or below the structures.

The Corps of Engineers has experimented with the replenishment of eroded shorelines by pumping sand from offshore areas to the original beach area with hydraulic dredges and pumps. This type of construction is effective in rebuilding the original beach but is very expensive and may only last until the next storm. However, one or more of the above techniques may be warranted if a more suitable site is not available.

The suitability of a beach site is also dependent on the availability of land for support facilities, such as parking areas, a bathhouse, and adequate road access.

*Inland-lake beaches.*   Inland-lake beaches are usually smaller than coastal beaches and fall into two categories: (1) natural lake beaches and (2) constructed lake beaches. Natural lake swimming beaches should be located at sites with suitable underwater conditions free from sudden grade changes, holes, drop-offs, and obstructions. A natural sand beach and an adequate land area for supporting facilities are other important site selection criteria. In most cases where natural lake beaches are located at sites that meet the above criteria, little or no underwater construction is necessary.[4]

Lakes developed primarily for flood control, water supply, or hydroelectric power production usually involve considerable earth moving and other construction to create a suitable beach area. In most cases it is necessary to grade the underwater area prior to filling the lake. Natural sand areas are seldom available, requiring the hauling and spreading of sand on the

PHOTO 5.1   *A natural beach site with adequate space for bathers and support facilities.*

Photograph courtesy of Miami-Dade, Florida Parks and Recreation.

beach itself and in the underwater area where water depth will permit wading (usually up to six feet). In constructing a beach at a man-made lake, consideration must be given to water level changes due to water storage and drawdown.

The construction of a swimming beach on lakes and reservoirs should be considered only after a study of all environmental factors such as wind and wave action, current, siltation, algae and underwater weed growth, and water quality has been made. Unfortunately, many of those factors are difficult to predict for a lake that has not yet been constructed. The Soil Conservation Service should be consulted relative to the control of upstream and on-site siltation. Local health department officials can determine pollution levels of feeder streams that will fill the proposed lake or reservoir. State and local health departments have laws governing acceptable water quality for swimming. As a result, it is impo tant to solicit their advice regarding general water quality as well as potential problems that might be associated with a specific shoreline site. The beach developer should be aware that public health agencies have the authority to close swimming areas where water quality falls below an acceptable level. While systems exist for improving water quality through chlorination, circulation, and aeration, they are expensive and difficult to control. If water quality problems are anticipated, the developing agency might be better off in constructing a swimming pool rather than a beach.

The best location for a lake-front swimming beach is where natural water currents and prevailing winds will provide a continuous circulation of fresh water to the site from the main body of the lake. The beach site should not be located too close to original streambeds, for those areas normally develop fast-moving currents during periods of high water that can easily wash out a sand beach and create hazardous conditions for swimmers.

*River beaches.* In general, the problems associated with the development of a river-front beach are of enough concern that a swimming pool is a better alternative. The biggest problem at river beaches is that they are subject to extreme water fluctuation and currents that can cause underwater changes in the bottom to occur. It is normally impossible to maintain a sand bottom, and silt and debris are often washed into the site.

If the river water quality is excellent and if flooding conditions are rare occurrences, a river-front beach may be realistic. A concrete bottom may have to substitute for sand, and structures may have to be constructed to protect the swimming area from current flows. Another alternative is to dredge a swimming basin adjacent to the river with an inlet and outlet to utilize the river current to circulate the water through the constructed site (see Figure 5.1).

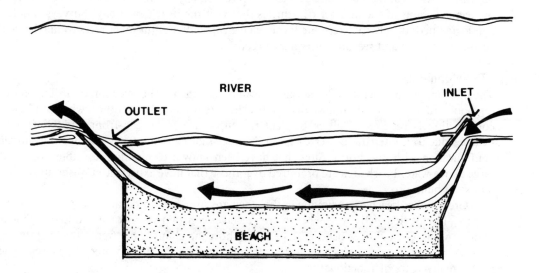

**FIGURE 5.1** *Dredged beach area adjacent to river takes advantage of natural current to circulate water.*

## Spacial Standards

The recommended beach area required for each visitor varies greatly. Some states determine space standards for swimming beaches while others do not. Local public agencies with large beach operations may develop their own specific spacial standards to control the number of swimmers using the beach at any one time, while others leave it up to the visitor to determine whether it is overcrowded. Table 5.1 recommends a breakdown of the space required at various types of beaches with the water area separated from the beach area. It also recommends space standards for recreation space, such as picnic and play areas, located behind but adjacent to the beach area.

TABLE 5.1   *Space Requirements of Beach Areas*

| | Square Feet Needed per Person | | | |
| Type of Area | Water | Beach | Back Up & Buffer | Total |
|---|---|---|---|---|
| High Density | 30* | 45 | 400 | 475 |
| Medium Density | 40 | 60 | 800 | 900 |
| Low Density | 60 | 90 | 1200 | 1350 |
| *20 minimum | | | | |

*Source:* Fogg, George E., *Park Planning Guidelines Revised* (Alexandria, Va.: National Recreation and Park Association, 1981), p. 118.

Spacial standards can be utilized in several ways: (1) to determine the number of life-guards and the type of life-saving equipment needed at a beach; (2) to determine the capacity of the beach area at any particular time; and (3) as an aid to planners in determining requirements for support facilities, (e.g., parking, restrooms, etc.). Beach planners and managers should also recognize that the daily capacity of a beach area is significantly greater than the capacity at any one time. Research indicates that each vehicle will average 3½ to 4 people and that there will be a turnover rate of two vehicles per day. Utilizing the preceding information, planners can fairly accurately determine the capacity of the beach by controlling the amount of parking provided at the site. Managers can get a reasonably accurate idea of total daily visitors by keeping count of the number of vehicles that visit the beach each day. Surveys should be conducted periodically to determine local vehicle capacity and turnover rates to maximize the accuracy of daily and seasonal attendance reports.

## Beach Development

The most important factor in developing a swimming beach is the selection of a site. On existing bodies of water, sites that have natural beaches are preferred over others where underwater construction is required. This is particularly important for ocean-front and Great Lakes beaches due to the terrific power of natural forces that can completely change the shoreline configuration with one storm. Sites that have been known to maintain a stable slope and a large above-water beach area are preferred over those that have experienced washouts, erosion, and sand build-up.

Great Lakes beaches are unique in that they are subjected to ocean-type wave action but, due to a lack of tidal activity, the beach area receives constant wave force at one shoreline elevation. Many Great Lakes beaches experience shoreline changes of twenty to thirty feet per year. As a result it is advisable to select a site with a very deep above-water beach area to help assure many years of functional use.

Once a site has been selected for a coastal or Great Lakes swimming beach, the primary concern is with the development of above-water facilities such as parking, bathhouse, and other considerations. Ocean-front beaches are confronted with the problem of stabilizing shifting sands caused by winds. A short-term solution may be found in the use of snow fencing to baffle the wind and deposit the sand on the beach where it is desired rather than on walkways, parking areas, and in buildings. A more permanent solution may be in the planting of pine trees, beach grass (ammophila), and other plants that can tolerate the harsh beach environment. Beach grass will not tolerate abuse from walking but is excellent for stabilizing beaches that are exposed to constant wind action. It may be necessary to construct elevated wooden walkways to protect stabilized beach areas from the destruction caused by arriving and departing swimmers.

PHOTO 5.2 *Elevated wooden walkways and ramps provide easy beach access and protects stabilized dunes.*

Photograph courtesy of Stone & Associates, Ft. Lauderdale, Florida.

Some ocean-front and Great Lakes beaches have been created by using dredges and pumps to move large quantities of sand from the off shore bottom to the proposed beach area. This technique is only successful if natural sand is available near the site, and because of the cost involved, it is usually done only at larger beaches in highly populated areas. Pumping sand from an offshore area to the shoreline should be avoided whenever possible, particularly when creating a new beach. The void left where the sand is pumped from often results in the shoreline deposit washing back out to level out the bottom. On the other hand, the replenishment of an existing beach area that is washed out as a result of a storm is an option worth considering.

The construction of swimming beaches on man-made lakes and reservoirs designed for flood control, water supply, or hydroelectric power production must consider water level drawdown in the development plan. Ideally, the site should have suitable topography, both above water and under water, to avoid large-scale earth movement. However, if the topography is not suited for a swimming beach, an artificial beach can be constructed by moving earth in sufficient quantities. Other problems to consider are siltation and pollution from the water supply. Where either situation exists the problem must be corrected at its source or it will be of little value to construct a beach. The advice and assistance of state and local health authorities should be secured before any beach development is considered.

Other major considerations in selecting a site for a beach development are as follows:

1. *Location.* The beach should be located close to a permanent or seasonal population; particularly at a commercial recreation development. In general, the greater the population base, the larger the beach and support facilities will have to be.
2. *Accessibility.* The proposed beach site must be easily accessible to the citizens it is designed to serve. If existing access roads do not exist or are inadequate, their construction will have to be included in the development plan.
3. *Climatic conditions.* The minimum water temperature should be in the upper 60s during the swimming season.
4. *Water quality.* The bacteriological quality should be less than 100 coliform per 100 ml. of water. Other potential pollutants such as industrial and agricultural wastes should be determined.
5. The site should be oriented to the sun for maximum warmth and sunbathing. However, some shade should be available for those wishing to escape the heat of the sun.[5]

## Underwater Construction

The swimming area should be cleared of all stumps, rocks, posts, and other objects. Then it should be graded smooth. In most cases involving the construction of a reservoir, this was done prior to filling the impoundment with water. On inland lakes and reservoirs it may be necessary to remove topsoil prior to spreading sand over the site. The Soil Conservation Service should be consulted to determine whether it will be necessary to prepare a base to keep mud from working up through the sand. It may be necessary to compact the existing bottom material, spreading a layer of gravel, or applying a layer of polyethylene to keep the sand separated from the bottom material.

Other underwater construction considerations involve surfacing material and slope.

*Surfacing material.*   Sand is the most commonly used underwater surfacing material for artificial lakes. It is relatively inexpensive if purchased locally and should be spread to a twelve-inch depth to a point where the water is six feet deep.

*Slope.*   The slope of the beach should begin well above the shoreline and continue to a water depth of at least six feet. The underwater slope should be between 5 and 10 percent with 7 percent being ideal. Sand placed on slopes of 8 or 10 percent will wash to deeper water requiring frequent replenishment or replacement.

## Above-Water Construction

Coastal swimming beaches utilize the natural slope and material found at the site. For lakes and reservoirs, however, it is necessary to address both considerations.

The slope of the above-water surface should be between 2 and 7 percent with 5 percent being ideal. The sand should be at least twelve inches deep and extend far enough up the beach to accommodate normal water level fluctuation. This might be as little as ten feet or as much as forty or fifty feet. This area is used a lot by small children and by swimmers entering or exiting the water.

The next 50 to 200 feet comprise the general use zone for sunbathing, relaxation, and casual play. Most artificial beaches provide turf as a surface material in the general use zone and a concrete retaining wall as a separation from the sand beach. The retaining wall might allow as little as four inches or as much as eighteen inches vertical distance from the sand to the turf area. The retaining wall helps keep the sand out of the turf which facilitates proper maintenance of each area and avoids the development of a muddy transition area.

PHOTO 5.3   *A wide, gently sloping beach allows room for a variety of activities.*

Crandon Park Beach. Photograph courtesy of Miami-Metro Parks and Recreation.

In northern climates where the potential exists for the retaining wall to be destroyed by ice movement, the lake side of the wall should be constructed at a 45-degree slope. This permits the ice to slide up and over the wall harmlessly rather than build up pressure against the face of the wall itself.[6]

### Support Facilities

The range of facilities found at swimming beaches varies widely, depending on the mission of the managing agency or organization, the population being served, the availability of financial resources, and the physical characteristics of land and water areas. Common to nearly all beach operations, however, are parking facilities, a bathhouse, and a concession area.

*Parking facilities.*   The largest amount of space at a swimming beach is that taken up by parking. The combined water and beach space needs for swimmers range between 75 and 150 square feet per person, while each vehicle needs approximately 300 square feet for parking and maneuvering within the parking facility. A general guideline for parking of standard size and compact cars is 150 cars per acre. At an average of 3½ to 4 persons per car, a one-acre parking facility can accommodate between 525 and 600 swimmers at any one time, which is not a particularly large beach operation. If several acres of parking are necessary, it is wise to develop several small parking areas that are designed to fit into the site rather than one large shopping-center-type facility.

Swimming beach managers who limit the number of visitors they feel can be accommodated safely at any one time can use parking availability to determine how many additional swimmers will be permitted to enter the area. On the other hand, large ocean-front public beaches may have an adequate beach area but are reluctant or unable to provide enough paved parking to handle a peak weekend or holiday crowd. Overflow parking fields might be made available to meet infrequent peak crowd days without the expense, not to mention the unsightliness, of large paved areas that would be empty on most days.

Walkways from the beach entrance area to the parking facility should be paved with a nonheat-absorbing material. Concrete, for example, is light in color and therefore does not get as hot as asphalt paving.

*Bathhouse.* The majority of today's beach visitors arrive at the beach by automobile already wearing their bathing attire. One investigation determined that only 8 percent of beach users require bathhouse facilities.[7] This is quite a departure from earlier days when the family arrived at the beach with a packed picnic basket, a change of clothes, towels, blankets, and folding chairs. As a result, the modern bathhouse does not have to be an elaborate facility.

The bathhouse should be centrally located so as to funnel visitors from the parking area to a minimal number of entrances to the beach. At beaches where a fee is charged, all swimmers may be required to enter through a single control area located in the bathhouse.

The size and use areas of a bathhouse should reflect the particular needs of each particular beach development. Typical use areas include the control center, clothes-changing facilities, restrooms, and a food and beverage concession.

Bathhouses should be constructed of durable materials such as concrete, brick, and stone that can withstand the continual exposure to natural forces. The building should be functional and designed to fit the site.

The type and quantity of plumbing fixtures required for a beach will vary from one area to another. Table 5.2 provides guidelines that should be used unless the local regulatory authority has more stringent requirements.

TABLE 5.2  *Plumbing Fixtures Required for Natural Bathing Places*

| Number of Fixtures | Commodes | | Urinals (Males) | Lavatory Per Sex | Showers Per Sex |
|---|---|---|---|---|---|
| | Male | Female | | | |
| 1 | 1-199 | 1-99 | 1-199 | 1-199 | 1-199 |
| 2 | 200-399 | 100-199 | 200-399 | 200-399 | 100-199 |
| 3 | 400-600 | 200-399 | 400-600 | 400-750 | 200-299 |
| 4 | | 400-600 | | | |
| | Over 600, one fixture for each additional 300 males and females. | | Over 600, one fixture for each 300 males. | Over 750, one for each additional 500 persons. | Over 299, one for each additional 100 persons. |

Note: From U.S. Public Health Service, *Environmental Health Practice in Recreation Areas,* Washington, D.C., HEW Publication No. (CDC) 78-8351, 1978, p. 49.

Nearly all beach areas operate food and beverage concession areas of some type. Operated properly, certain concessions can generate a significant amount of revenue to help recover other expenses associated with a beach operation.

Food and beverage concessions should stay with a relatively simple menu of items that are quick and easy to prepare, and that do not create unnecessary safety or maintenance problems. Beverages should be sold in paper cups or cans. All glass containers should be avoided for ob-

**PHOTO 5.4** *An attractive and functional concession area overlooking the public beach at Boynton Beach, Florida.*

Photograph courtesy of Stone & Associates, Ft. Lauderdale, Florida.

vious safety reasons. Straws should not be provided for drinks due to the difficulty in recovering them from sand beaches, even with mechanized beach rakes.

Three additional support facilities that are commonly found at public beaches are picnic areas, casual or structured play areas, and children's playgrounds. All can be compatible with a swimming beach complex and add to the enjoyment of the experience. Playgrounds, in particular, can play an important role in attracting young children there instead of to the water.

## BEACH OPERATIONS

While basic operating procedures are similar for both ocean-front and other types of swimming beaches, each has certain necessary management activities that are unique to that particular setting. The unique operational procedures of ocean-front or Great Lakes beaches as compared to inland-lake beaches are due to differences in size, number of swimmers, water conditions, and marine hazards.

Inland-lake beaches are seldom more then several hundred feet in length while coastal beaches may extend for several miles. It is not uncommon to charge an admission fee to enter a lake swimming beach, which can be profitable. It is less common to charge such fees at coastal beaches. The concentration of large numbers of swimmers can be equally as great at either type of beach, but ocean-front beaches that extend for long distances have a unique problem in providing guard services for swimmers dispersed along the shoreline.

Marine conditions at inland-lake as well as coastal beaches are dynamic and not always obvious from a shoreline vantage point. Inland-lake beaches have to deal with turbid water,

**PHOTO 5.5**  *A shaded sitting area is a popular addition to any swimming beach.*

Photograph courtesy of Stone & Associates, Ft. Lauderdale, Florida.

levels of coliform, and other pollutants, and underwater changes due to currents, flooding, and debris washing into the swimming area. Managers of ocean-front beaches must contend with surf, tide, and current flows; great distances between guard stations; and various forms of marine life. Ocean-front and Great Lake beaches often utilize mechanical beach cleaners to remove litter, aquatic weeds, and other debris from the sand, while the primary maintenance concern relative to inland lakes may be to maintain a healthy stand of turf in a sunbathing area under poor growing conditions.

**PHOTO 5.6**  *The Barber Surf-Rake removing the debris at Gateway National Park Recreation Area.*

Photograph courtesy of H. Barber & Sons, Inc., Bridgeport, Connecticut.

In addition to the standard qualifications required of all lifeguards, the ocean-front guard must possess specialized knowledge and skills necessary for the unique problems that can develop from the coastal marine environment. Ocean-front lifeguards must be proficient in long-distance surf swimming and in the efficient use of specialized life-saving equipment such as surfboats and surfboards. They must be able to recognize potential dangers resulting from changes in wave and current patterns that might cause undertows, riptides, and changes in bottom contour. The ocean-front lifeguard must also be familiar with various forms of marine life, knowledgeable of potential dangers each might present, and know the appropriate first aid procedure to treat various stings, bites, and other injuries.

## STAFF

The most obvious member of the swimming beach staff is the lifeguard. His presence is obvious and his activities are critical to a successful beach operation. Except for extreme southern states and California, the position of lifeguard is seasonal and usually occupied by college students and teachers. Public beaches in Florida and California are exceptions in that their lifeguards are often highly trained and experienced full-time employees who take pride in their unique profession.

A large agency with multiple aquatic facilities may hire a full-time person with the title of Aquatics Director to oversee the operation of pools, beaches, marinas, lakes, and other water-based facilities. The primary concern of this chapter will focus more specifically on the staff requirements for a single swimming beach rather than on an entire aquatics operation.

Large swimming beach operations will find it necessary to have multiple job classifications for lifeguards. Newly hired guards might assume the position classification of Lifeguard I, with more experienced guards having the title of Lifeguard II or Lifeguard Captain. The following position descriptions are based on those required by the Boynton Beach, Florida, Recreation and Park Department. They are not appropriate for every beach operation but may be of value in developing job requirements that reflect the unique characteristics of a particular facility.

### Lifeguard Captain

This person has overall responsibility for the protection of life on a beach. He is responsible for the enforcement of all rules and regulations governing lifeguard and public activity and for all reporting data relative to the beach operation.

*Qualifications:* A minimum of four years paid experience as a professional ocean lifeguard in a municipal, county, or state recreation department. A minimum of two consecutive years experience as a professional ocean lifeguard in the beach division of a municipal or county recreation and park department. Thorough knowledge of life-saving methods and practices and of life-saving equipment. Must possess a current valid Senior Life-saving certificate, although a Water Safety Instructor (WSI) certificate is preferable.

*General duties and responsibilities:*
1. Responsible for all phases of the lifeguard operation.
2. Responsible for training and supervising all lifeguards.
3. Responsible for maintaining training and performance records of individual lifeguards.
4. Responsible for all record keeping and reporting as mandated by the operating agency.

### Lifeguard II

This person is responsible for the general observation and supervision of the beach area, and for the safety of persons on the beach or in the water.

*Qualifications:* Thorough knowledge and competence in the following areas:

1. Ocean currents and ocean current rescue procedures.
2. Basic rescue techniques.
3. Artificial respiration.
4. Long-distance and rough-water swimming.
5. Swimmer education relative to the prevention of various ocean-front dangers.
6. Personnel supervision.
7. Lifeguard physical training and conditioning.
8. First aid.
9. Public and employee relations.
10. Red Cross Life-saving certification.

*Desirable experience and training:*
1. Three years experience as Lifeguard I.
2. Completion of an oceanic rescue training course.
3. Possession of a valid Red Cross Life-saving certificate.
4. High school graduate.

*General duties and responsibilities:*
1. Responsible for Lifeguard I supervision.
2. Responsible for all beach activities in the absence of the Beach Captain.
3. Responsible for maintaining self and Lifeguard I staff in top physical condition.
4. Responsible for guarding and safety activities as directed by the Beach Captain.

## Lifeguard I

This person's primary responsibility is beach observation and safety. Work consists of performing life-saving functions and preventative safety measures. He works under the supervision of the Lifeguard Captain or Lifeguard II.

*Qualifications:* Thorough knowledge and competence in the following areas:

1. Basic rescue techniques.
2. Ocean currents and ocean current rescue techniques.
3. Artificial respiration.
4. Long-distance and rough-water swimming.
5. Public and employee relations.
6. Appropriate personal appearance and behavior.
7. First aid.

*Desirable experience and training:*
1. Completion of an oceanic rescue training course.
2. Possession of a valid Red Cross Life-saving certificate.
3. Lifeguard experience.
4. High school graduate.

## General Rules of Conduct

Employees of a public beach are observed by more citizens on a continual basis than other agency employees. Because of the environment in which beach employees work, it is important to be aware of how citizens perceive the actions of each staff member. The following are suggestions for assuring a positive image:

1. Take breaks out of the public eye.
2. Always present a neat and clean appearance wearing proper uniforms.
3. Smile and greet beach users with courtesy.

4. Do not argue with visitors. Refer complaints and problems to the proper supervisor using the chain of command as appropriate.
5. Be alert, active, and moving. Do not lounge around reading newspapers, books, etc.
6. Do not spend long periods of time conversing with patrons. Be courteous and answer questions, but keep moving.
7. Do not allow users in guard stations or loitering around stations.

Rules of conduct for lifeguards are very much the same regardless of the type or location of the beach. Some of the more common are as follows:

1. No lifeguard shall report for duty or be on duty under the influence or in possession of any intoxicant or drug.
2. Guards must report to their assigned post at the assigned time.
3. Guards must not participate in any form of gambling activity while on duty.
4. Guards are not to be insubordinate or use abusive language to a co-worker, supervisor or public.
5. Lifeguard stands must be operated with all proper equipment as determined by the lifeguard captain or beach supervisor.
6. Guards are not to accept responsibility for watching personal items or baby-sitting.
7. The public shall be treated in a courteous and professional manner.

Penalties may vary for violations of these rules, depending on the seriousness and circumstances under which each takes place. Penalties may range from a verbal warning to written reprimand, suspension, demotion, or discharge. Penalties should be consistent with agency or governmental unit policies.

## Beach Patrol Procedures

Procedures must be developed to provide a high level of consistency in the quality of lifeguard and safety services. The following examples are required of ocean-front lifeguards in Boynton Beach, Florida:

### Beach Patrol Rules:

As a Boynton Beach Lifeguard you will be expected to maintain the highest degree of professionalism concerning the skills and attitudes which must be maintained in order to provide a Beach Patrol of the highest calibre. Certain regulations and policies have been developed to insure this high level of service.

1. *Station Assignments:*
   At the beginning of the work day, the Beach Supervisor will assign each lifeguard to a specific station or stand. These assignments are made on the basis of currents, marine hazards, and density of crowds in a given area. These assignments may change during a work day as the previously mentioned conditions may change.
2. *Relief and Breaks:*
   Relief may be requested for short rest periods and will be granted, as conditions allow, by the Beach Supervisor. Under no circumstances is the lifeguard to leave the boundaries of the public beach, picnic, or parking area without the consent of the Beach Supervisor. Relief requests shall be made using the intercom system. A guard shall not leave his assigned station until a request has been approved and a relief guard arrives to assume his area of responsibility.
3. *Attentiveness:*
   The nature of duties of an Ocean Lifeguard demand a high level of attentiveness. Anything which distracts or impairs the ability of the guard to maintain this level is not in keeping with the high standards competent lifeguards must maintain. Lifeguards shall not read books or magazines while on duty and swimmers are present. Long conversations are to be discouraged. No one but authorized personnel is allowed in or on the guard stand and equipment room. The ability of one to see his entire area of responsibility is essential. Vision should not be blocked by

windbreakers, umbrellas, etc. Beach patrons should not be allowed to impair the lifeguard's vision of, or access to swimming areas with umbrellas, windbreakers, chairs, etc.

4. *General Appearance:*
Each lifeguard is responsible for the neatness and general appearance of area to which he is assigned. Cans, bottles, paper, driftwood, etc., shall be removed. Even more important than the general appearance aspect is the safety factor. Cans, bottles, driftwood, and sharp objects of any sort can be the source of many sorts of serious injuries.

## LIFE-SAVING EQUIPMENT

The choice of life-saving equipment depends to a great extent on the character of the beach, local water conditions, and the number of lifeguards assigned to a given area. The following is an overview of the type of safety equipment commonly found at major public beaches:

1. Lifeguard chairs or towers at an elevation of at least six to seven feet above the beach allow an unobstructed view of the area to which they are assigned. The lower section of the chair or tower can be designed to contain first aid and safety equipment. An information board placed on the back is valuable in posting current beach and bathing conditions (e.g., temperatures, tides, currents, marine pests, etc.).
2. Resuscitators or inhalators should be convenient to all guard personnel. Coastal beaches often assign a resuscitator-inhalator unit to each guard tower. They should be checked daily to assure they will be in proper working order when needed.
3. Advisory flags allow lifeguards to warn bathers of dangers which may exist on a given day in a given area. A simple but functional procedure is the "traffic light" system. A green flag denotes good swimming; yellow indicates the presence of water conditions which may not be conducive to comfortable and safe swimming; red indicates hazardous bathing conditions. Swimming should not be permitted when the red flag is flown.
4. Torpedo buoys carried to a victim by a lifeguard are used to support the troubled swimmer while being towed in by the lifeguards remaining on the beach.
5. First aid kits should be readily available to all lifeguards for the treatment of victims of sudden illness or accidental injury. First aid kits should be kept well stocked and orderly.
6. Rescue or paddle boards are particularly valuable in making long-distance assists or rescues, and should be readily available to all guards.
7. Telephones or two-way radios are important items at extensive beach operations. Either can be used to communicate with the central office, first aid station, police, or other lifeguards. Portable two-way radios can be carried while on foot patrol or even while in rescue boats.
8. Lifeboats have proven to be valuable for offshore patrol of swimming areas and for rescues in strong currents and rough seas. They should be positioned at a central location on the beach near the waterline during on-duty hours and equipped with oars and other items necessary for rescue and patrol.
9. Binoculars are necessary for lifeguards guarding large coastal beaches but usually unnecessary for those guarding inland-lake swimming facilities. They are particularly valuable for interpreting a situation occurring a good distance from the lifeguards' stations.
10. Bullhorns are useful in getting the attention of swimmers over the sound of surf or crowd noise.

## BEACH REGULATIONS

Beach regulations are developed for the health and safety of all swimmers. Generally speaking, the more crowded the area, and the greater the potential dangers in the water, the more it is necessary to provide restrictions on visitors' activities. Specific rules and regulations should not be adopted unless there is good reason to believe their absence could result in accident, injury, or the inconvenience of others. The following are samples of regulations that have been established at beaches in various sections of the United States. To avoid lengthy explanation, each is preceded by an emphatic NO ...

- littering, peddling, advertising, pets, or fires.
- bikes or skateboards on boardwalks.
- sitting on railings.
- surfing or fishing in swimming areas.
- tents or shelters other than umbrellas.
- boats to be launched or beached.
- swimming near jetties or piers.

These regulations, and more, can be found at extensive municipal or county beaches. Inland-lake beaches would have different and probably fewer regulations. Regulations should be prominently posted for patrons to see as they enter the beach area to avoid confusion and constant reprimands from lifeguards.

# BEACH SAFETY

Many water accidents occur within easy reach of safety. Most ocean-front beach rescues are a result of swimmers becoming caught in riptides and littoral currents that develop quite suddenly and carry a person out toward open water or parallel to the shore for great distances.

Common safety problems at inland-lake beaches involve swimmers stepping in a hole, accidently getting into water that is too deep, weak swimmers needing help, overestimating ability, or being struck by an object or another person.

A constant concern at all beaches is for children who wander away from their parents, resulting in the parents becoming frantic that the child is in the water. An immediate search of the water becomes necessary which tends to upset many of the other swimmers. A wise lifeguard captain will have someone look for the child at nearby play facilities and in restrooms, concession areas, and the parking lot while the underwater search is in progress.

Many inland-lake beaches clear the water for ten minutes every hour or two to give the swimmers and lifeguards an opportunity to rest and give families a chance to regroup.

### Emergency Procedures

Emergency situations are inevitable, though preventative lifeguarding can minimize the frequency and severity of occurrences. When a rescue must be made, the guard staff must respond promptly and in an efficient and well-coordinated effort.

While each emergency situation seems to have unique circumstances, experience has provided guidelines for responding to most incidents. The major safety concerns at coastal beaches involve hydrological conditions such as runouts, undertows, set or wind currents, and jetties or breakwaters.

Runouts are created by a buildup of water on the beach side of a sandbar. When the sandbar can no longer hold back the pressure of the water, a break occurs in the sandbar creating a runout. A runout is similar to a fast-moving stream that dissipates once past the sandbar.

When rescuing a swimmer carried to open water by this condition, the lifeguard can use the power of the runout to get to the victim. If the rescue is made by boat or surfboard, the return to shore is made back through the runout. If the lifeguard must swim to the victim, the return to shore is made over the sandbar (see Figure 5.3).

Undertows are caused through the deposit of water from waves upon the beach that flow back out beneath on-coming waves (see Figure 5.4). Undertows vary in strength and length

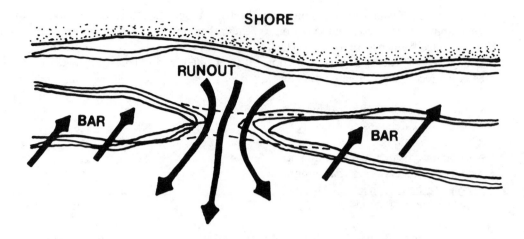

**FIGURE 5.3** *Hydrological formation of runouts.*

Adapted from Gabrielson, M.A., B. Spears, and B.W. Gabrielson, *Aquatics Handbook,* 2nd Edition, Prentice-Hall, Englewood Cliffs, N.J.: 1968, p. 234.

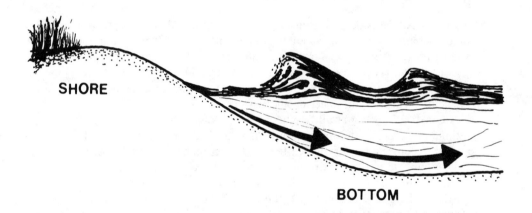

**FIGURE 5.4** *Short, steep beach causes a powerful undertow.*

Adapted from Gabrielson, M.A., B. Spears, and B.W. Gabrielson, *Aquatics Handbook,* 2nd Edition, Prentice-Hall, Englewood Cliffs, N.J.: 1968, p. 235.

depending on the contour of the beach and the size of the waves. Drop-offs can be made by the undertow washing sand down the beach and dropping it right under the breaking point of the waves.[8] Lifeguards should return undertow victims to the beach by swimming parallel to the shoreline in the direction of the current until the danger is passed, then in to the beach.

Set or wind currents are caused by the current running in the same general direction of the wind. Lifeguards should not fight the current but instead swim the victim with the current while gradually working toward the beach.

Jetties and breakwaters can be potentially dangerous areas when combined with set or wind currents. The current will not only flow into the structure but may cause whirlpool-type currents. The best escape from this situation is to swim out around the breakwater or jetty and into the beach on the other side (see Figure 5.5).

Major safety concerns at inland-lake beaches may seem simple in comparison to ocean-front beaches, but such is not the case. Changes in bottom conditions can develop that are not

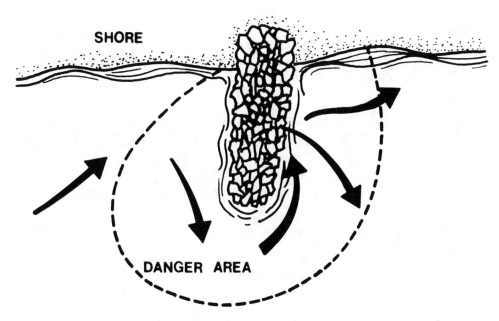

**FIGURE 5.5** *The current around jetties and breakwaters creates dangerous hydrological conditions.*

Adapted from Gabrielson, M.A., B. Spears, and B.W. Gabrielson, *Aquatics Handbook,* 2nd Edition, Prentice-Hall, Englewood Cliffs, N.J.: 1968, p. 235.

apparent on the water's surface. Holes and drop-offs can develop from sand washing into deeper water, submerged logs can be washed into the beach area, and careless swimmers can overestimate their ability. The lifeguard staff can minimize those and other occurrences through daily in-water inspections of the bottom, safety lines, and raft structures. Swimmer rules should prohibit the use of floats or other objects that might provide a false sense of security or accidentally hit an unsuspecting swimmer.

Floating lines should delineate the boundary of the swimming area as well as separate the use areas. The beginning swimming and wading zone extends from the shoreline outward to approximately 3½ feet in depth or less. The general swimming zone extends from there to about the 6-foot depth. If a diving platform is provided, it should be separated from the general swimming zone and have at least 10 feet of water depth extending out from the raft at least 20 feet.

If use is heavy in the general swimming zone or diving area, guard chairs may be mounted on floating platforms at the perimeter of those zones.

Clearing the water for a short period every hour or two is a good safety policy and allows an opportunity for the staff to demonstrate aquatic skills and safety procedures.

## SUMMARY

This chapter has attempted to discuss the important considerations in developing and managing swimming beach facilities that will help guarantee safe and enjoyable participation. Many common management problems can be avoided through the selection of an appropriate site and the development of a quality swimming beach complex. The beach staff must be carefully selected, well trained, and sensitive to the needs of the public with whom they come in contact. Finally, the manager must give high priority to the safety, comfort, and enjoyment of the swimming beach patron.

# NOTES

1. Gabrielson, M.A., B. Spears, and B.W. Gabrielson, *Aquatics Handbook,* 2d Edition (Englewood Cliffs, N.J.: Prentice-Hall, 1968), p. 227.

2. *Ibid.,* p. 33.

3. Wright, David G. "Public Beaches," A Manual and Survey on Construction and Operation," *Management Aid Bulletin No. 51* (Alexandria, Va.: National Recreation and Park Association, 1965), p. 6.

4. *Ibid.,* p. 7.

5. Jubenville, Alan, *Outdoor Recreation Planning* (Philadelphia, Pa.: W.B. Saunders Co., 1976), pp. 234–36.

6. Wright, "Public Beaches," p. 16.

7. *Ibid.,* p. 19.

8. Gabrielson, *Aquatics Handbook,* p. 234.

# BIBLIOGRAPHY

Bureau of Outdoor Recreation. *Guidelines for Understanding and Determining Optimum Recreation Carrying Capacity.* Washington, D.C.: Department of the Interior, 1977.

Chamberlain, Clinton J. *Marinas: Recommendations for Design Construction and Management,* vol. 1. Chicago: National Marine Manufacturers Association, 1985.

Cordell, H. Ken, and John C. Hendee. *Renewable Resources Recreation in the United States: Supply, Demand and Critical Policy Issues.* Washington, D.C.: American Forestry Association, 1982.

*Encyclopedia of Associations.* 19th ed. Detroit: Gale Research Company, 1985.

Fogg, George E. *Park Planning Guidelines Revised.* Alexandria, Va.: National Recreation and Park Association, 1981.

Gabrielson, M.A., B. Spears, and B.W. Gabrielson, *Aquatics Handbook.* 2d ed. Englewood Cliffs, N.J.: Prentice-Hall, 1968.

Hall, Norville, L. "Manual and Survey on Small Lake Management," *Management Aid Bulletin No. 8.* Alexandria, Va.: National Recreation and Park Association, 1961.

Heritage Conservation and Recreation Service. *The Third Nationwide Recreation Plan.* Washington, D.C.: U.S. Department of the Interior, 1979.

Jubenville, Alan. *Outdoor Recreation Planning.* Philadelphia: W.B. Saunders Co., 1976.

Knudson, Douglas M., *Outdoor Recreation.* New York: Macmillan Publishing Co., 1980.

Kraus, Richard. *Recreation and Leisure in Modern Society,* 3d ed. Glenview, Ill.: Scott, Foresman and Company, 1984.

Moran, Henry. *Marina, Finance to Function.* Raleigh: Revenue Sources Management School, North Carolina State University, 1968.

National Association of Engine and Boat Manufacturers. *Boat Handling Equipment in the Modern Marina,* 1959.

_____. *Marina Costs/Revenue Study,* 1974.

_____. *Marina Operations and Services,* 1967.

_____. *The Modern Marina,* 1963.

Sternloff, Robert, and Roger Warren. *Park and Recreation Maintenance Management.* 2d ed. New York: Macmillan Publishing Co., 1984.

Szmedra, Philip, E.E. Brown, and R.M. North. *Feasibility for Dry-Stack Boat Storage at the Georgia Coast.* Athens, Ga.: University of Georgia, Research Bulletin 298, 1983.

Toubier, Joachim, and Richard Westmacott. *Lakes and Ponds*. Urban Land Institute, Technical Bulletin No. 72, 1976.

U.S. Army Corps of Engineers. *National Shoreline Study*. Washington, D.C.: Department of the Army, 1971.

U.S. Coast Guard. *Boating Safety Manual*. Washington, D.C.: U.S. Department of Transportation, 1984.

U.S. Congress, Senate Committee on Commerce. *Legislative History of the Coastal Zone Management Act of 1972*, 1972.

U.S. Department of Agriculture. *1981 Program Report and Environmental Impact Statement*. 1981.

_____. "Ponds for Water Supply and Recreation," *Agricultural Handbook No. 387*. Washington, D.C.: Soil Conservation Service, 1971.

_____. *Recreation Ready Reference*. Broomall, Pa.: Northeast Technical Service Center, Soil Conservation Service, 1977.

_____. *Warm-Water Fishponds*. Washington, D.C.: Farmers' Bulletin No. 2250, 1977.

U.S. Environmental Protection Agency. *Coastal Marinas Assessment Guidance Handbook*. Atlanta: U.S. Environmental Protection Agency, 1984.

U.S. Public Health Service. *Environmental Health Practice in Recreation Areas*. Washington, D.C.: HEW Publication No. (CDC) 78-8351, 1978.

Warren, Roger, and Philip Rea, *Swimming Pool Management*. Columbus, Ohio: Publishing Horizons, 1985.

Wright, David G., "Public Beaches, A Manual and Survey on Construction and Operation," *Management Aid Bulletin No. 51*. Alexandria, Va.: National Recreation and Park Association, 1965.